Old Wine in New Bottles

Modern Russian Anti-Proverbs

Andrey Reznikov

"Proverbium"
In cooperation with the
Department of German and Russian

The University of Vermont
Burlington, Vermont
2009

Supplement Series

of

Proverbium
Yearbook of International Proverb Scholarship

Edited by Wolfgang Mieder

Volume 27

Cover design: Boris Burakov

ISBN 978-0-9817122-1-5

Manufactured in the United States of America
By Queen City Printers Inc.
Burlington, Vermont

For my wife Irina

Contents

Acknowledgments..vii

Preface..ix

1. Introductory Notes..1

2. Major Patterns of Anti-Proverbs......................7
   Pattern I. Similar form – same wisdom..........7
   Pattern II. Similar form – new wisdom..........18
   Pattern III. Extension of the traditional
        proverb....................................50
   Pattern IV. New form – new wisdom.............71

3. Soviet Anti-Proverbs....................................84

4. Language Mechanisms Used in Creating Anti-
   Proverbs...................................96
        Phonetic mechanisms.......................98
        Morphological mechanisms.................104
        Lexical mechanisms........................107
        Syntactic mechanisms.....................115
        Stylistic mechanisms......................118
        Defeated expectancy 124
        Combination of different mechanisms ...128

5. Conclusion: Anti-Proverbs or Modern Proverbs?.......131

Appendix: Index of Anti-Proverbs.....................133

Notes..169

Bibliography...177
.

Acknowledgments

I would like to thank all the known and unknown authors who created anti-proverbs analyzed in the book: without their wit and wisdom my research would be impossible.

The research was partially supported by a grant from the Faculty Research Committee, Black Hills State University, and I would like to thank the committee members for their support of my work.

Last but not least, I wish to express my deepest gratitude to Professor Wolfgang Mieder, chairperson of the Department of German and Russian at the University of Vermont: not only do I owe him the idea of this book but I am also grateful for his encouragement and valuable advice during all the years of my work on the manuscript. He also was kind enough to provide helpful editorial suggestions.

Andrey Reznikov

Petrozavodsk, Russia – Spearfish, South Dakota
2006 – 2008

Preface

You probably have never heard the anti-proverb, *A timely confession turneth away the wrath of the reader*. The reason for that is very simple – I made it up, in order to warn my readers what this book is *not* about.

This is not a book that sets its goal as further development of the theory of paremiology, or suggesting a new concept of proverbs and sayings. This is not a book where the reader will find a detailed history of paremiological studies in this country or abroad, either. In short, the book does not pretend to be a new word in theoretical studies.

Instead, this book offers a detailed language analysis and examination of modern Russian anti-proverbs, based on the corpus of 6,000 examples, and this analysis is carried out in many aspects: the form of anti-proverbs, their meaning, their relationships with the traditional proverbs, and last but not least, their chances for survival in the Russian language. All this makes the book unique, as it is the first research that offers scrupulous linguistic analysis of modern Russian anti-proverbs and language means that are used in the process of their formation, as well as analysis of their status in the modern Russian language and culture.

The corpus of examples is classified into four major patterns, depending on the correlation between the form and the meaning of the traditional proverb and its new version, that is, the anti-proverb:

1. *Similar form – same wisdom*
2. *Similar form – new wisdom*
3. *Extension of the traditional proverb*
4. *New form – new wisdom*

Since one of the key questions concerning anti-proverbs is the question of their future – that is, whether they will stay in the language and become respectable proverbs, or whether they will

X

disappear – a special chapter is devoted to examining the anti-proverbs of the soviet period in the Russian language (1917-1991), as this material may give some hints about the future of modern anti-proverbs.

In the appendix, there is a list of all anti-proverbs analyzed in the book, with their traditional prototypes and English equivalents, where they exist, as well as a brief description of the language mechanism(s) used in their formation.

And no man putteth new wine into old bottles;
else the new wine will burst the bottles,
and be spilled, and the bottles shall perish.
Luke 5:37

Старая пословица с новым веком ссорится
(Old proverbs quarrel with the new era)
A 20th century Russian proverb

1. Introductory Notes

Status of Anti-Proverbs

Before discussing modern Russian anti-proverbs, we need to define them, at least, preliminarily.

The term "anti-proverbs" (Antisprichwort) was coined by Wolfgang Mieder and it is widely accepted in paremiological studies all over the world. Professor Mieder defined anti-proverbs (AP) as "deliberate proverb innovations (alterations, parodies, transformations, variations, wisecracks, fractured proverbs)" (Litovkina 5). Thus, the definition of AP is based on the definition of proverbs (that which is being altered, transformed, etc.), so we need to define the proverbs first.

This task is far from easy. The specialists in the field know very well that there is not a single accepted definition of proverb that would satisfy everyone. At the same time, there are often quoted (and thus attaining the proverbial status themselves) classical definitions, for example, the definition of Barlett Jere Whiting given in his 1932 article "On the Nature of Proverbs":

> A proverb is an expression which, owing its birth to the people, testifies to its origin in form and phrase. It expresses what is apparently a fundamental truth – that is, a truism, – in homely language, often adorned, however, with alliteration and rhyme. It is usually short, but need not be; it is usually true, but need not be. Some proverbs have both a literal and figurative meaning, either of which makes perfect sense; but

2

more often they have but one of the two. A proverb must be venerable; it must bear the sign of antiquity; and, since such signs may be counterfeited by a clever literary man, it should be attested in different places at different times. This last requirement we must often waive in dealing with very early literature, where the material at our disposal is incomplete (quoted from Mieder 2004, 2)

As well-written and venerable this extended definition may be, it can hardly be used as a practical tool in my research, though it does show the problems of even a working definition. Without discussing in detail all the existing attempts to define proverbs (there is extensive bibliography on that topic[1]) I will use, as a working definition, the definition of Wolfgang Mieder which is given in his handbook *Proverbs:*

Proverbs are concise traditional statements of apparent truths with currency among the folk. More elaborately stated, proverbs are short, generally known sentences of the folk that contain wisdom, truths, morals, and traditional views in a metaphorical, fixed, and memorizable form and that are handed down from generation to generation. (4)

Thus, proverbs are statements that are:

- Apparent truths and traditional views (wisdom, truth, morals)
- Popular among native speakers
- Metaphorical, fixed and memorizable in form
- Handed down from generation to generation.

Consequently, anti-proverbs should be *deliberate innovations of concise traditional statements of apparent truths with currency among the folk.* Hence, an obvious question should be asked next: what aspect(s) of proverbs is (are) being innovated in anti-proverbs? The meaning (apparent truths)? The form? Both meaning and form? (Obviously, popularity and dissemination cannot be "innovated"; these things anti-proverbs should share with proverbs in order to be known, if at all).

Main Types of Anti-Proverbs

Depending on the possible combinations of innovations, I tentatively divide all the anti-proverbs into four major patterns:

1. *Similar form - same wisdom*
2. *Similar from – new wisdom*
3. *Extension of the traditional proverb*
4. *New form – new wisdom*

Similar/new form can range from the change of one letter/sound on the one hand and up to a completely new lexical content of the same syntactic structure, on the other. A detailed analysis of all language mechanisms used in creating anti-proverbs is given in Chapter IV.

What is *new wisdom*? It is well-known that the vast majority of traditional proverbs have two layers of meaning: literal and figurative. For example, *As you sow you shall reap*. Obviously, it means, first, what it says: depending on how well (or how poorly) you sow your crops you will get either a good harvest or a poor harvest. But it also has a figurative meaning, which is much more valuable: the results of your actions depend on how well (or how poorly) you do something, not necessarily sowing crops, but it can be doing anything else. In other words, in any sphere, if one wants to get good results one should act accordingly.[2]

Thus, by new wisdom in anti-proverbs I will mean either or both of the two new meanings: either a new literal meaning, or a new figurative meaning.

With these ideas in mind, let us now start the analysis of modern Russian anti-proverbs. To classify the material, I will use the main patterns of correlation between the form and the meaning in anti-proverbs (AP) and their prototypes, traditional proverbs (TP), listed above. Within each pattern, I further subdivide the material into broad semantic groups:

- New political and economic realities
- Health and medicine
- Relationships between sexes
- Drinking
- Language jokes (wordplay)

It is important to keep in mind that such sub-classification cannot but be tentative: for instance, an anti-proverb reflecting new realities may, at the same time, be a joke or belong to the group of health and medicine, or describe relationships between sexes. While deciding how to classify any particular anti-proverb, I tried to take into account its major emphasis, though I certainly realize that such a classification, as any semantic classification, is inevitably subjective. Finally, not all of the patterns exhibit examples in all five categories.

I should also point out that the term *traditional proverb* is used in a broad sense here: it includes not only proverbial expressions per se, but also lines from popular songs, famous quotations from Russian and foreign authors, well-known slogans, etc.

A Brief Survey of Modern Scholarship on Anti-Proverbs in Different Languages

Numerous collections of anti-proverbs in various languages have been published since Wolfgang Mieder and Lutz Röhrich published their book *Sprichwort* (1977), where the term *anti-proverb* (Antisprichwort) was used for the first time. Before long this triggered an interest of paremiologists in this phenomenon, and the first publications started to appear. Many of them contain detailed surveys of the literature on this subject, and I can refer the reader to some of the most recent ones; for example, the survey that is given in the Introduction to the dictionary *Anti-Proverbs of the Russian People* (Walter, Mokienko 2005), as well as the survey given in one of the latest publications by Professor Mieder, *Anti-Proverbs and Mass Communication* (2007,

18-19). The most extensive bibliography on the subject is given in the Introduction to the latest collection of AP in English, *Old Proverbs never Die, They just Diversify* (Litovkina, Mieder 2006). The Introduction itself is an example of careful multi-aspect analysis of modern English anti-proverbs (2-54).

The latest, to the best of my knowledge, collection of research papers dedicated to the phenomenon of anti-proverbs in different languages was published in 2007, when *Acta Ethnographica Hungarica*, an international journal of ethnography, dedicated a special volume to the study of anti-proverbs. It contains articles analyzing this phenomenon in such different languages as German, Hungarian, French, English, Dutch, and Russian. At the same time, most of them follow the tradition of earlier research and discuss the anti-proverb (and proverb) phenomenon through some specific aspect: for example, humor in Hungarian anti-proverbs (Boronkai, Litovkina), usage of proverbs and anti-proverbs (Vargha, Litovkina), anti-proverbs and their lexicographical description (Walter, Mokienko), proverbs in wellerisms (Carson), compound French proverbs (Barta), French anti-proverbs about food and drink (Barta), pragmatic aspect of Bulgarian anti-proverbs (Hristova-Gotthard), and phonetic means of Dutch anti-proverbs on the Internet (Predota).

The only exception to this general rule is the extensive paper published by four researchers (Litovkina, Vargha, Barta, Hristova-Gotthard) about the most frequent types of alteration in Anglo-American, German, French, Russian and Hungarian anti-proverbs (47-105). Unfortunately, too general a topic and too wide a scope of diverse languages does not allow the researchers to provide a detailed analysis, or suggest a meaningful classification of the types of alterations. Still, in my opinion, such an approach is clearly the first stop in the right direction. Here, I could not agree more with professor Mieder who wrote in his paper "Anti-Proverbs and Mass Communication": "Collections and textual/linguistic studies do not suffice. We must also look at where and how the anti-proverbs exist and live and how at least some of them become *bona fide* proverbs! <…> There is a clear lack of serious field research in proverb studies at the present time, both regarding traditional proverbs and creative anti-proverbs" (19).

And this is exactly the main goal of my book – to fill this gap in the area of modern Russian anti-proverbs.

Obviously, such research would be impossible if the first step had not been already made – that is, if there were no collections of Russian anti-proverbs. There are two dictionaries of Russian AP published by now (summer 2008): Walter, H., Mokienko V. *Anti-poslovitsy russkogo naroda* (Anti-Proverbs of the Russian People). Neva publishers, 2005); and Mokienko V., Walter, H. *Pricolny slovar* (Dictionary of Jokes: Anti-Proverbs and Anti-Aphorisms). Neva Publishers, 2006 (6,000 anti-proverbs). Besides, about 60 new proverbs of the soviet period are recorded in the *Dictionary of the Soviet Language* (Mokienko V., Nikitina N. *Tolkovy slovar yazyka sovdepii.* Saint-Petersburg University Press, 1998).

2. Major Patterns of Anti-Proverbs

Pattern I. Similar Form – Same Wisdom

It is common knowledge that many traditional proverbs are synonymous, that is, contain the same general truth or folk wisdom. So at first sight it is not surprising that anti-proverbs can do the same, that is, preserve an old truth, but express it in a new form. But a more in-depth analysis shows that this pattern is far from being merely one more proof of the synonymous nature of the folk wisdom. The peculiarity of anti-proverbs of this type is the fact that they contain *modern day realities*, and thus, were not possible in earlier days. Let us have a look at some of the most interesting and at the same time typical examples. I tentatively classify them into two semantic groups: anti-proverbs reflecting new realities of modern-day Russia (and expressing old wisdom through new ideas) and language jokes (wordplays), again, preserving old truths.

A. New Political and Economic Realities

(1)
TP: *Куй железо, пока горячо.* (Strike the iron while it is hot). Figuratively, it means that one should do something while the timing is right.

AP: *Куй железо, пока Горбачев* (Strike the iron while Gorbachev). The figurative meaning is the same as the figurative meaning of the traditional proverb.

The literal meaning of the traditional proverb is obviously taken from the work of the blacksmiths. The meaning of the AP, at first sight, makes little sense: what is the connection between working the iron and it being while Gorbachev is in power? But because the AP clearly associates in the minds of the Russian speakers with the traditional proverb, it is obvious that the real (figurative meaning) of AP is the same: do something while the time is right (or it will be too late, as it is late to work the iron when it is cold). In other words, use the opportunities of perestroika.

The form of the AP is homophonic with the form of the TP: the Russian words *горячо* (hot) and *Горбачев* (Gorbachev) rhyme (they differ in one phoneme only, as the name *Горбачев* has one more phoneme, phoneme [b]), which makes the association with the traditional proverb even stronger and clearer.

(2)

TP: *Волков бояться в – лес не ходить* (If you are afraid of wolves do not go to the forest). Figuratively, it means that if you are afraid of taking risks do not do risky things, or, in other words, risks are part of achieving something in life. Literal meaning is absent.

AP: *Путина бояться – в сортир не ходить* (If you are afraid of Putin, do not go to the outhouse).

The most interesting feature of this AP is that its figurative meaning is exactly the same as the one of the traditional proverb; but the origin of the wording is of course quite new: it is an allusion to the famous Putin's promise "to kill terrorists everywhere, including outhouses."[3]

The association with the TP is achieved, in this case, not by similarity in sound, but by the similarity of the morphological and syntactic structure: the AP uses the same syntactic frame, with the same two verbs in the same form: *If you are afraid of___, do not go to ___.* But that is not all: since the meaning of the AP is the same as that of TP, the words *Путин* (Putin) and *сортир* (outhouse), that replaced the original *волки* (wolves) and *лес* (forest) respectively, by that very replacement have become contextual synonyms to the words that they substituted: *Putin* and *wolves* (as symbolizing something to be afraid of) and *forest* and *outhouse* (as symbolizing some scary place).

(3)

TP: *Долг платежом красен* (The debt is made red by the payment). The literal meaning is that one should promptly return the money one owes to somebody. Figuratively, it can also mean that anything that you owe someone (not necessarily money) should be promptly returned.

AP: *Долг платежом зелен* (The debt is made green by the payment). The literal meaning is the same; figurative meaning is absent.

Now, why, of all things, are *green* and *red* used in these proverbs? The answer is different in each case. For the traditional proverb, it is explained by the old meaning of the adjective *red*, which used to mean "beautiful, good looking" (thus, for instance, Red Square in Moscow is, of course, "beautiful square," not square red in color). Thus, *the debt is made red by the payment* means that it is good (morally correct) to pay your debts, both monetary and others.

Green is quite opposite in its etymology, and originates in the realities of modern Russian economy, where the dollar is the most reliable currency[4] (unlike ruble, which, especially in the early 90-s, due to hyperinflation, was not used in commercial transactions). Since dollar bills are green, the AP uses metonymy and in fact says that one should pay one's debts in dollars. The peculiarity of this particular AP is that at the same time, due to the literal meaning of the adjectives *red* and *green* (as colors) it is a great example of the play on words, where there are two levels of meaning (in fact, three), which create the play. Thus, there are at least two language mechanisms at play in this modern Russian anti-proverb: metonymy and polysemy (twice).

(4)
TP: *Храните деньги в сберегательных кассах!* (Keep your money in the savings banks!) Figurative meaning is absent. This is a well-known advertisement of the soviet times (together with such ads as "Fly Aeroflot!" etc.) The irony of these and similar soviet slogans is that it is not a true advertisement, as Savings Bank was the only bank anyway, so there was no choice where to keep your money; the same is true about Aeroflot, which was the only airline available to the soviet citizens.

AP: *Храните деньги в сберегательных баксах!* (Keep your money in the savings bucks!)

Obviously, this is one more saying reflecting modern Russian realities (in this aspect it is similar to the previous one), where keeping one's money in US dollars (i.e., bucks) is the safest way to protect your savings from inflation. Linguistically, the

AP is very well coined: the syntactic structure is the same, and the Russian words банках (*banks*) and баксах (*bucks*) rhyme, thus reminding everyone (or at least every person who lived in the soviet times) of the original saying.

(5)
TP: *Гусь свинье не товарищ* (A goose and a pig cannot be friends). Figuratively, persons from different spheres of life cannot have anything in common.
AP: *Евро баксу не товарищ* (Euro and dollar cannot be friends). Figurative meaning is absent.

Once again, the anti-proverb, using the syntactical pattern of the traditional proverb, expresses the same idea by means of the new realities, because in the sphere of economic relationships, the euro (that is, European economy) and the dollar (that is, US economy) are competitors, not friends. The association of the AP and the TP is achieved by the same syntactic frame and partly the same wording: *.... cannot be friends.* Besides, this is a great example of one of the versions of metonymy, *pars pro toto*: part (dollar, euro) representing whole (economy).

(6)
TP: *Дружба дружбой, а табачок врозь* (Though we are friends, I am not going to share my tobacco with you). Figuratively, it means that there are limits to what friends will do for each other.
AP: *Дружба дружбой, а нефть врозь* (Though we are friends, I am not going to share my oil with you). Figurative meaning is absent.

The AP is another reflection of modern Russian realities, where oil companies compete for oil deposits and federal government support. The association with the traditional proverb is achieved by the same syntactic pattern and common wording, except one word: *oil* (in AP) as opposed to *tobacco* in the TP. The use of the word *табак* (tobacco) in TP is not accidental: it reflects the traditional high value of tobacco in Russia, hence, unwillingness to share it even with friends.

Oil in modern Russia is as valuable a possession as tobacco was in old days. Thus, it is one more example of contextual synonymy, and chances are, if the AP survives it may develop the figurative meaning, as well.

(7)

TP: *Семь бед – один ответ* (Seven problems – one answer). Figuratively, it means that one will have to answer for all the mistakes or wrong actions, no matter how many, once only. This is similar to English, *You die only once.*

AP: *Семь бед – один reset* (Seven problems – one reset). Figurative meaning is absent.

This AP is obviously a part of modern computer slang, as it talks specifically about computer problems: no matter how many you have, there is one universal answer to any and all of them: reset. It is important to mention that the word *reset* is written in English in the Russian AP, which is typical of computer slang, based to a large extent on English terms.[5]

Besides, the AP rhymes with the TP: the Russian word *ответ* (answer) rhymes with *reset*, thus establishing a clear association with the TP; finally, TP and AP have the same wording and structure, except one word.

(8)

TP: *Скажи мне, кто твой друг, и я скажу тебе, кто ты* (Tell me who your friend is, and I will tell you who you are). Thus, the people who are one's friends describe one as a person; judging by your friends one can learn something about you. There is hardly any figurative meaning in this TP.

AP: *Скажи мне, что ты ешь, и я скажу тебе, кто ты* (Tell me what you eat, and I will tell you who you are). Thus, the things you eat tell others about your social status; figurative meaning is absent.

One more time, the anti-proverb reflects modern Russian realities: the rich and the poor in modern-day Russia eat widely different things; so judging by the food one eats it is really possible to define one's status in life.[6] The association with the TP is clear by the syntactic structure, and also by the same wording, except the first subordinate clause: *Tell me .... and I will tell you who you are.*

(9)

TP: *Ниже пояса не бить* (Do not hit below the belt). This is one of the rules of the honest fight; figuratively, it can also mean any kind of "fight" which is done according to established rules, not necessarily physical fighting.

AP: *Ниже пейджера не бить* (Do not hit below the pager); the meaning is the same, as a pager is kept on the belt.

This is an interesting example of new wording for a traditional wisdom; the association is made clear by some phonetic similarity of the Russian words *пояс* (belt) and *пейджер* (pager), the same syntactic structure, and the same verb: *Ниже _____ не бить* (Do not hit below ____). Besides, the words *пояс* (belt) *пейджер* (pager) are used as contextual synonyms, as they both indicate the same area of the human body.

(10)

TP: *По одежке встречают, по уму провожают* (One is greeted by the clothes, and seen off by the mind.) Figuratively, it is similar to the English saying *Appearances are deceptive*; *Beauty is only skin deep*, etc., thus, we first judge people by the way they look, and later on, when we learn more about them, we judge them by their inner world.

AP: *По прикиду встречают, по понятиям провожают.* (One is greeted by the clothes, and seen off by the street laws). The meaning is very much the same, but stylistically the wording is completely different. First, it has the word *прикид* for the word *clothes*; this word belongs to prison slang. Secondly, instead of *mind*, the AP uses the term *по понятиям*, which can be roughly described as a set of unwritten criminal street laws and rules used in relationships between criminal groups. The association with the original proverb is achieved by preserving the structure and both verbs of the original proverb: *По _____ встречают, по _____ провожают* (One is greeted by____, one is seen off by____), though stylistically the AP belongs to the low colloquial register, having replaced the key nouns by their stylistic synonyms.

(11)

AP: *Не говори гоп, пока не перепрыгнешь* (Do not say "gop"[done] until you jump over). This traditional Russian proverb is similar in its wisdom to the English proverb, *There is many a slip between the cup and the lip*. It tells us not to boast about having done something until we actually have done it.

TP: *Не говори гоп, пока не переедешь Чоп* (Do not say "gop" until you pass Chop).

Chop is a small city on the border between Ukraine and Slovakia. The border guards in Chop are known for their thorough searches of the people crossing the border. Hence, the moral of this new version in a way repeats the old truth, though making it more concrete: do not think you crossed the border until you passed the border patrol in Chop. The new version has internal rhyme, which makes it especially good, as internal rhyme is a standard feature of many old Russian proverbs. In fact, in this aspect it is better than the old version, as the latter does not have internal rhyme.

(12)

TP: *Двое пашут, а семеро руками машут* (Two people are plowing, and seven people are waving hands). This is a traditional Russian proverb, which means that fewer people are actually doing something than those who show how to do something.

AP: *Кто пашет, а кто с Мавзолея рукой машет* (Some are plowing, and some others are waving their hands from the Mausoleum).

This is an interesting version of the new saying preserving the old truth. The Mausoleum in this proverb is Lenin's mausoleum in Red Square in Moscow. It was used as the platform from which the soviet leaders greeted military parades and demonstrations of the people traditionally held in Red Square during big soviet holidays, especially during May 1 (Labor Day) and November 7 (Revolution Day). The new version preserves the internal rhyme that was used in the original proverb, but uses new realities to express the old wisdom.

B. Language Jokes (Wordplays)

(13)

TP: *Поживем – увидим* (We shall live and see). The figurative meaning is, we shall see what will happen; usually said to people who are very sure in their predictions of the results of their actions.

AP: *Пожуем – увидим* (We shall chew and see). The figurative meaning is the same, as chewing (that is, eating – a great example of metonymy) is, in its turn, part of living; so again, double metonymy, allowing the AP to preserve the original meaning, in spite of the change of one of the two verbs.

The peculiarity of this particular AP is that it is nearly 100% homophonic with the traditional proverb: the Russian verbs *поживем* ([we] *shall live*) and *пожуем* ([we] *shall chew*) coincide except for one phoneme; the second verb in both proverbs is the same; thus, the AP cannot but recall (and hence, being associated with) the traditional proverb.

(14)

TP: *Не переходите улицу на красный свет* (Do not cross the street when the light is red). This, in fact, is not so much a proverb as a well-known saying (traffic rule), one of those basic things that kids are taught in elementary school, hence, well-known to everyone. No figurative meaning is present in this saying.

AP: *Не переходите улицу на тот свет* (Do not cross the street to the other world). That is, if you cross the street when the light is red, you will get hit by the car and die.

The peculiarity and black humor of the AP is based on the play on words: the Russian words *light* and *world* are homonyms; hence, literally, (красный) *свет₁* (red) *light* and (тот) *свет₂* (the other) *world* sound and look the same. The association with the TP is based on the same syntactic structure and nearly same wording, except for one word: *красный* (red) in the TP and *тот* (other) in AP: *Не переходите улицу на _____ свет.* At the same time, as we can see, the AP not only preserves the meaning of the original expression, but even makes it stronger and more emphatic.

(15a)

TP: *Чем бы дитя ни тешилось, лишь бы не плакало* (Whatever the child plays with, the most important thing is that it does not cry). Thus, anything is worth allowing the child to do as long as it does not cry. Figuratively (and often ironically) said about adults who do something unusual or strange for a grown-up person, but like it anyway.

This TP is one of those cases when it gives origin not to one, but several AP; in fact, the *Dictionary of Jokes* lists 15 AP based on this proverb. Here are the two that I find most interesting linguistically:

AP: *Чем бы дитя ни тешилось, лишь бы не какало* (Whatever the child plays with, most important is that it does not poop). One need not try to look for some deep meaning here; it is just a language joke, based on the rhyming words *плакало* (cry) and *какало* (poop).

(15b)

AP-2: *Чем бы дитя ни тешилось, лишь бы не факалось* (Whatever the child plays with, most important is that it does not fuck).

This AP is interesting for several reasons. First of all, the Russian saying uses the English verb *fuck* in Russian transliteration and with Russian morphological endings of a Russian reflexive verb – as if it were a Russian verb. Secondly, the result is as low colloquially as the verb *fuck* is in English. Thirdly, even though quite rude in form, it very precisely reflects the biggest concern of most parents who have teenaged kids – thus, again, continuing the tradition of proverbs expressing the mores of the day.

(16)

TP: *Назвался груздем, полезай в кузов* (If you said you are a mushroom, get into the basket). This TP is used only figuratively: if you said you can do something, do it and do not complain; often said to someone who is complaining about his or her problems with something that this person is doing or is expected to do.

AP: *Назвался клизмой, полезай в попу* (If you said you are a clyster, get into the anus).

Again, although much more low in style and wording, this AP in fact preserves the figurative meaning of the original proverb. This is achieved, partly, through the similarity in structure and wording, so the AP reminds any native speaker of the traditional proverb: *Назвался ____, полезай в _____* (If you said you are a ____, get into ____).

(17)

TP: *Снявши голову, по волосам не плачут* (When you lost your head, you do not cry over your hair). This TP is used only figuratively: When you have a big problem, it is not the right time (or too late, it is no use) to worry about small problems.

AP: *Снявши штаны, по волосам не гладят* (When you took off your pants, you do not stroke [your girlfriend's] hair).

Surprisingly, the figurative meaning – or at least part of it – is basically the same: at such a moment you do something bigger than just stroking [your girlfriend's] hair. True, the AP is quite rude in its connotation, but it only reflects the modern times, so we should not blame the Russian language for that. AP is clearly associated with its traditional prototype by several things: the same syntactic structure, rhyming verbs (the Russian verbs *плачут* (cry) and *гладят* (stroke) rhyme), and last but not least, the play based on different meanings of polysemantic verb: *lost* and *took off* are two meanings of the same verb *снимать* (incidentally, both sayings use a morphologically archaic form of the verb – *снявши*).

Finally, a couple of examples of the lowering of the stylistic status of traditional sayings while preserving their meaning:

(18)

TP: *Счастливые часов не наблюдают* (The happy do not notice the time). Thus, the meaning is, when one is in love and is together with the beloved person, he or she does notice how much time passed.

This saying is a well-known quotation from the poem *Grief from the Mind* by Alexander Griboyedov, the famous Russian poet of the late 18th century. Incidentally, literally dozens of quotations from this poem are now part and parcel of the Russian language and have acquired truly proverbial status: many native speakers do not realize when they use these sayings that they are quoting Griboyedov.

AP: *Счастливые трусов не одевают* (The happy do not put on underpants).

Once again, even though the literal meaning is quite different and stylistically the AP is quite low, it does preserve at least part of the original meaning: happy lovers do not have time (which they do not notice anyway) or need to put on underwear as they make love all the time. The association with the TP is achieved by the same structure and rhyming of the replaced words (the Russian words *часов* (time) and *трусов* (underpants) rhyme; as well as the verbs *замечают* (notice) and *одевают* (put on).

(19)

TP: *Птицу видно по полету* (The bird is seen by its flight); used figuratively, one can judge a person by the way he or she acts.

AP: *Птицу видно по помету* (The bird is seen by its droppings).

This is a good example of a joke, since the Russian words *полету* (flight) and *помету* (droppings) rhyme, thus creating a humorous effect. But that is not all; even though it is first of all a joke, it does preserve the figurative meaning of the original saying: as one can define the type of person by the way he or she acts, so one can define the type of bird by its droppings. The association with the TP is achieved by the same structure and nearly the same form: only one phoneme is different in the Russian words *полет* (flight) *помет* (droppings): [l] is *полет* is replaced by [m] in *помет*.

18

Pattern II: Similar Form – New Wisdom

This group is by far the biggest among modern Russian anti-proverbs, and this is only natural: a typical AP using the association with the TP, which exists in the mind of the native speakers, fills the same syntactical and/or morphological and phonetic structure with a new meaning, which more often than not has nothing to do with the literal or figurative meaning of the original expression. Let us have a look at some examples that I find most interesting, both semantically and structurally. Since this group is the largest, it is no surprise that it has examples for all the five broad semantic groups mentioned earlier:

- New political and economic realities
- Relationships between sexes
- Drinking
- Health and medicine
- Language jokes (wordplays)

A. New Political and Economic Realities

This group, as the name shows, is the group which unites quite different anti-proverbs, but having one thing in common: they all reflect realities of the post-soviet Russia, whether good or bad. Most of these things or events were unheard of in the Soviet Union; hence, there could not be any proverbs based on them. These new realities are as diverse and as broad as scarcity of food during perestroika times, on the one hand, and up to new market economy and "new Russians" lives, on the other.

(20a)
TP: *Долг платежом красен* (The debt is made red by the payment).
I have already discussed this TP in the first section (#3); as we will see, it gives birth to more than one AP; just to remind the readers, it literally means: the debt is made red by the payment; the adjective "red" here preserves its old meaning of "beautiful"; in other words, it is good thing to do to pay your debts, all kind of debts, in time and in full. Figuratively, it can also mean that

anything that you owe someone (not necessarily money) should be promptly returned.

AP: *Долг утюгом страшен* (The debt is made scary by the iron).

It is hard to understand the meaning of this saying unless one lives in modern day Russia; the hint of the proverb is that if someone does not pay his debts, the people who gave him the money will come and threaten him with the hot iron until he returns the money. This may sound like a line from a bad horror movie, but it is an unfortunate part of modern day reality.

The association with the TP is achieved by the same structure, and by the rhyming words *красен* (red) and *страшен* (scary).

(20b)

AP: *Долг процентом красен* (The debt is made red by the interest).

The readers can guess, by now, that "red" here means "good." Again, it is a new reality of modern Russia: it is good not simply to pay one's debts (as it was said in the traditional proverb), but it is good to pay one's debts with interest. In this case, the association with the TP is achieved mostly by the same structure: the first and the third words are the same in both TP and AP; thus, they make up a frame in which the word *плате-жом* (payment) is replaced by the word *процентом* (interest).

(21)

TP: *Тише едешь – дальше будешь* (The slower you go, the farther you will get). This proverb is often used in its figurative meaning: if you do something without undue haste, you will manage to do more.

AP: *Водитель, помни: тише едешь – никому не должен* (Driver, remember: the slower you go, the less you owe to anyone).

The AP repeats the structure (and the first part verbatim) of the TP, but prefixes it with the introductory phrase, "Driver, remember." This is one more hint to modern day realities: if you drive too fast, you end up being stopped by the police and getting a speeding ticket; quite often to avoid that, the drivers would offer money to the police; hence, the slower you go, the less money you will pay.

(22)

TP: *Плачет девочка в автомате* (A girl is crying in the phone booth). This is not a traditional proverb, but a line from a very popular love song (lyrics by Andrey Voznesensky), about a young girl whose boyfriend does not want to see her anymore, so she is calling him from a pay-phone and crying.

AP: *Плачет девочка в банкомате* (A girl is crying near the ATM). The original line is clearly recognizable in this version, as not only the structure of the two sentences is the same, but also the Russian words *автомат* (phone-booth) and *банкомат* (ATM) rhyme.

Now, what about the meaning? Well, again, it has nothing to do with the original line; the girl is probably crying near an ATM because there is no money in her bank account; 20 years ago such a scene (and certainly, the phrase) was impossible simply because there were no ATMs in the Soviet Union.

(23a)

TP: *Аппетит приходит во время еды* (Appetite comes with eating; the original proverb is a calque from French *L'appetit vient en mangeant*). This proverb is also found English, *Appetite comes while eating*. The literal meaning is clear; but it can also have a figurative meaning: one really understands and starts to enjoy some vocation only when one is actually doing something.

AP: *Аппетит приходит вместо еды* (Appetite comes instead of eating).

Obviously, the figurative meaning is absent here, but the literal one reflects the sad reality: there can be nothing to eat, either because people have no money to buy food, or because, especially in transition time, there was scarcity of goods in grocery stores.[7]

The association with the TP is achieved by the same structure and nearly the same wording; in fact, only prepositions are different in the TP and AP: *во время* (with) in the traditional saying, and *вместо* (instead of) in the new version.

(23b)

AP: *Гепатит приходит во время еды* (Hepatitis comes with eating).

This time, the association with the original saying is achieved, first of all, by the phonetic similarity of the Russian nouns *аппетит* (appetite) and *гепатит* (hepatitis). This AP could be interpreted as a harmless lang-

uage joke, but it is not: it is a sad, but true fact that hepatitis comes with eating, and numerous cases of hepatitis (especially in day care centers and similar institutions for children) are proofs for that.

(24)

TP: *Мойте руки перед едой* (Wash your hands before eating). This is a well-known slogan propagating public hygiene, and known by everyone since one's childhood.

AP: *Мойте руки вместо еды* (Wash your hands instead of eating).

The meaning of this AP is very much similar to the previous one: if you have no food, all you can do is the first part of the procedure: washing your hands. The language device used here is also the same as in the previous example: the change of preposition: *перед* (before) is replaced by *вместо* (instead of).

(25)

TP: *Не зная броду, не суйся в воду* (If you do not know the place of the ford, do not go into the water; similar to the English, *Look before your leap*). The proverb obviously has a figurative meaning, too: If you are not sure of what you are doing or about to do, do not even start.

AP: *Не зная броду, не ври народу* (If you do not know the place of the ford, do not lie to your people).

Of course, this phrase has very little to do with the original saying (except that it has the same structure and rhymes with the TP), and reflects another aspect of modern-day Russia, this time, modern Russian politics: politicians often lie to the people, promising them things they will never be able to do; so the AP warns them about the consequences of this: sooner or later they will have to answer.[8]

22

(26)

TP: *В человеке все должно быть прекрасно: и лицо, и одежда, и душа, и мысли* (Everything must be beautiful in a man: the face, the clothes, the soul, and the thoughts). This is a well-known quotation from the play *Uncle Vanya* by Anton Chekhov. It will be recognized by any native speaker, and even though many people will not remember the author of this saying, they will know the saying itself; this, again, proves that this quote has acquired proverbial status in the modern Russian language.

AP: *В бизнесмене все должно быть прекрасно: и 600-й мерс, и дача на Канарах, и контрольный выстрел в голову* (Everything must be beautiful in a businessman: his Mercedes, his vacation home in Canary Islands, and his control bullet in the head).

There is another version of this AP, which differs only in the details, but preserves the same meaning (so I can analyze them together): *В бизнесмене все должно быть прекрасно: и костюм, и мобильник, и контрольный выстрел в голову* (Everything must be beautiful in a businessman: his suit, his cell phone, and his control bullet in the head). The association with the original saying is achieved mostly by the same structure: introductory phrase (Everything must be beautiful in a (business) man), and the list of the characteristics, although in the TP there are four of them, and in both versions of the AP – only three, but this is probably because of the fact that the wording for each of them is longer in AP, hence the overall structure and rhythm remains mostly the same.

Now, what about the meaning? I am repeating myself, but again, one has to live in Russia today to understand this strange sentence. The thing is, that much of modern business is criminalized; rivalry is often resolved not by market means and honest competition but by bullets. So no one is guaranteed against being killed, and no matter how rich you are (Mercedes, vacation home in Canary Islands) no one can feel safe. The second wording is more modest in describing the attributes of a rich person (suit, cell phone), but it should be kept in mind that some short time ago a cell phone in Russia was so expensive that only very rich people could afford it. (Now, of course, the situation has changed, and cell phones are everywhere).

(27)

TP: *Почем опиум для народа?* (How much is opium for the people?)

Contrary to what it looks like, this saying is not about drugs or drug-dealers. This is a quotation from a famous novel by two soviet writers, Ilya Ilf and Evgeniy Petrov, *Twelve Chairs*. The plot takes place after the revolution in soviet Russia; several characters of the novel are trying to find the treasure hidden in one of the twelve chairs; obviously, everyone wants to find it before the others. One of the contenders is a priest, so he is teased by this phrase, "How much is opium for the people?" This is a hidden hint to his profession: it is, in its turn, an allusion to the famous definition of religion by Carl Marx, who called it *opium of the people* ("*das Opium des Volkes*") in his work *Zur Kritik der Hegelschen Rechtsphilosophie* (1844). Thus, when other characters in the novel tease the priest with this phrase, they hint that it is unworthy for a priest to be chasing money.

AP: *Почем пентиум для народа?* (How much is Pentium for the people?)

This saying has very little to do with the original TP, except its form: it not only repeats the original sentence, but the words *opium* and *Pentium*, both in Russian and in English, rhyme. As for the meaning, it is for a change quite obvious: how affordable are computers for average people. One should not look for any deep meaning here, but as long as the association with the TP is alive (and it is, since the novel is well known even today, partly thanks to several popular screen versions, based on the book), the AP has good chances of staying in the language.

(28a)

TP: *Не имей сто рублей, а имей сто друзей* (Do not have a hundred rubles, but have a hundred friends). The meaning is quite obvious: a hundred friends will help you much more than a hundred rubles. This proverb gave birth to two AP, one of them appeared during the Soviet Union times, and the other one is much younger.

AP: *Не имей сто рублей, а женись как Аджубей* (Do not have a hundred rubles, but marry as Adjubey did).

Alexey Adjubey was a soviet journalist who married the daughter of Nikita Khrushchev, General Secretary (this position was called First Secretary in those days) of the Communist Party of the Soviet Union (1953-1964). Obviously, Adjubey made an amazing carrier, and was appointed editor-in-chief of a major daily newspaper in the USSR, *Izvestia*.

The association with the original proverb is achieved by several things; first of all; both TP and AP have internal rhyme: *рублей* (rubles) and *друзей* (friends) in the TP, *рублей* (rubles) and *Аджубей* (Adjubey) in the AP. Secondly, they have the same syntactic structure and share the first clause: *Не имей сто рублей, а...* (Do not have a hundred rubles, but ...)

(28b)

AP: *Не имей сто рублей, а имей сто баксов* (Do not have a hundred rubles, but have a hundred bucks).

This is one more proverb which reflects modern day realities: it is sad but true that US dollars (i.e., bucks) are preferred to rubles, as a safe way to save one's money. (Incidentally, these days, when the dollar is weak and euro is strong, it is slowly changing, and most people prefer euros, but there is no corresponding version of this proverb so far).

Linguistically, this version is worse than the previous one: there is no internal rhyme, as there is in the original proverb, so the only thing that connects this proverb with the original sentence is the structure. Since rhyme (and rhythm) is a key element of many traditional Russian proverbs, we can safely predict that this AP will not stay in the language, unlike its predecessor (28a), which has been in the Russian language for several decades.

(29)

TP: *Счастье – это когда тебя понимают* (Happiness – it is when you are understood). This sentence is a well-known phrase from a popular soviet film *Let Us Live till Monday* (1968).

This movie is about a senior class in a high school; the students were given the assignment to write an essay on the topic, "What Is Happiness?" One of them gave this answer: "Happiness is when you are understood by others."

AP: *Переоценка ценностей: счастье – это когда тебя нанимают* (Change of values: happiness – it is when you are hired).

The introductory phrase that appears in the new version is pretty straight-forward: really, in the market economy in today's Russia, with a substantial unemployment rate, it is happiness to have a job.

Linguistically, the AP is very well coined: it not only repeats the structure of the TP (which is usual), but phonetically is nearly the same: only one phoneme is different in the Russian words *понимают* (understood) and *нанимают* (hired): [p] in the first verb, and [n] in the second.

(30)
TP: *Хочешь жить – умей вертеться.* (If you want to live, you should be able to spin). This is quite a pragmatic old wisdom: if you want to live in the real world, you should be prepared to do all it takes to survive and prosper.

AP: *Хочешь жить – умей раздеться* (If you want to live, you should be able to undress). This AP pushes the old pragmatic maxim to a new, cynical, extreme, reflecting another sad reality: it is an open secret that often the career of a pretty girl or woman depends on whether she is willing to provide sexual favors to her boss.

The association with the original saying is achieved by the familiar combination of factors: the same structure and rhyming verbs in the original saying: *вертеться* (spin) and *раздеться* (undress) in the new version.

(31)
TP: *И скучно, и грустно, и некому руку подать* (I am bored, and sad, and have no one to shake hands with).

This is the first line from a well-known poem of the great Russian poet Michael Lermontov (1814-1841), describing his loneliness in the Russian society of his days.

AP: *И скучно, и грустно, и некому тело продать* (I am bored, and sad, and have no one to sell my body to).

As we can see, the meaning of the AP has nothing to do with the original saying, although it does repeat its structure and rhymes with the TP: the verbs *подать* (shake) and *продать* (sell) not only rhyme, but in fact differ only in one phoneme: the latter one has one more phoneme, phoneme [r].

(32)
TP: *Точность – вежливость королей* (Accuracy is the politeness of the kings). This saying allegedly belongs to the French king Lois XVIII. It is quite popular in the modern Russian language and society.
AP: *Точность – вежливость снайперов* (Accuracy is the politeness of the snipers).

This saying could be interpreted as merely a harmless language joke, but it does reflect an aspect of the modern Russian society, when assassinations of well-known political or business people are done by professional killers. Linguistically the new coinage is not ideal: *королей* (kings) and *снайперов* (snipers) do not rhyme; thus, the association is achieved only by the structure; besides, rhythmically the TP and AP are also different, as the Russian word *kings* has its stress on the last syllable, while the Russian word *snipers* has its stress on the first syllable (though both are three-syllable words in Russian).

Now let us have a look at another AP, with the similar meaning, but which is a much better coinage linguistically.

(33)
TP: *Язык до Киева доведет* (Talking will get you to Kiev). This is an old proverb which means that if you ask people the way you can get anywhere by asking (it is important to keep in mind that Kiev was not just part of Old Russia, but for a long time it was the political center of the country).
AP: *Язык до киллера доведет* (Talking will get you to a killer [i.e., get killed]). The meaning is, obviously, that if you talk too much you will get into trouble. Here, not only the structure and rhythm of the TP and AP are the same, but even phonetically they are very close: *Kiev* and *killer*, being paronymous,

even though different in phonetic structure, do sound very similar in Russian.

(34)

TP: *Будешь много знать – скоро состаришься* (If you know too much you will get old quickly). This is an old saying, usually said to people who like to poke their noses into other people's business, or simply ask too many (silly) questions; often said to kids, too.

AP: *Будешь много знать – не успеешь состариться* (If you know too much you will not be able to get old).

If the TP is more like a kind joke, the AP is far from it: it is a serious warning, and the meaning is quite similar to the meaning of the previous entry: it is dangerous to know too much. It is clearly associated with its traditional prototype both by the structure and nearly the same wording: *скоро* (quickly) in the TP is replaced by *не успеешь* (will not be able) in the AP.

(35)

TP: *Богата талантами земля наша!* (Rich in talents is our land!) This is a traditional saying claiming that many Russian people are talented.

AP: *Богата зарытыми талантами земля наша!* (Rich in buried talents is our land!) As we can see, the meaning is quite different: our country is rich in people whose talents are wasted. This change is achieved by inserting a modifier *зарытыми* (buried) before the noun *talents*.

Another interesting linguistic aspect of the AP is that, unlike its TP prototype, the AP is associated with the biblical parable about the buried talent (Matthew 25:25), thanks to the homonymous nature of the words *talent* as a gift for something and *talent* as a coin, both in Russian and in English.

(36)

TP: *Автомобиль не роскошь, а средство передвижения* (The automobile is not a luxury but a means of transportation.)

This is another proverb originating in the novel *Twelve Chairs*, discussed in #27, and cannot be understood without knowing the context. The main heroes of the novel, who are chasing the treasure, are traveling in an old car. At one point they travel along the route of an auto rally, designed to educate the population about automobiles (the plot takes place in the early 20s of the 20th century, when cars were rare). They pretend to be the first car of the rally, and are greeted (and fed) by crowds of people, so they have to make some short speeches. Hence, their leader says: "The automobile is not a luxury but just a means of transportation." Since the time this novel was published, this phrase has become well-known (partly because in the Soviet Union times the automobile *was* a luxury), and is often used.

AP: *Народ не роскошь, а средство обогащения* (People are not a luxury but a means of getting rich).

The original proverb is recognized by anyone who has read the novel (or has seen an equally popular movie based on the novel) in this version, which of course reflects the modern Russian realities: the rich get richer, the general population gets poorer. The association with the TP is achieved by the same syntax and by the fact that the words *обогащения* (getting richer) in the AP and *передвижения* (transportation) in the TP rhyme.

(37)

TP: *Худой мир лучше доброй ссоры* (Bad peace is better than a good quarrel; similar to the English proverb, *A bad compromise is better than a good lawsuit*). The meaning of this traditional proverb is clear: peace is always better than war, even if its conditions may be not as good as one would like.

AP: *Худой «Мир» лучше доброго «Челленджера»* (Bad "Mir" is better than good "Challenger").

The meaning is quite different, and of course is based on the play on words. First of all, at the first layer of meaning, so to speak, it is a hint to well-known facts: the Russian space station *Mir*, which was outdated and whose existence had to be terminated, still served its purpose longer and better (even though being comparatively "bad") than the modern shuttle *Challenger* who had a fatal accident during its tenth launch on January 28, 1986. But this is only the first, factual layer; another one is that the Russian words for *peace* and *world* sound the same [mir]; in the names of the space station, obviously, the word "world" is used, but thanks to its homophonic nature with the word "peace" the first part of the AP sounds (though does not look, due to the quotation marks and capital letter) like the traditional proverb: [*hudoi mir luchshe…*], thus establishing a clear association with the TP, though, again, having very little to do with its meaning. Thus, this AP is a very good example of both linguistic means used to create a clear association with the TP (a must for any AP) and a reflection of modern-day realities.

(38)

TP: *Редкая птица долетит до середины Днепра* (It is a rare bird that can fly till the middle of the Dnepr river). This is a well-known description of the Dnepr River from the novel *Dead Souls* by Nikolay Gogol. This phrase, though it has no figurative meaning, is often cited as a great example of the description of nature in the classic Russian literature.

AP: *Редкий премьер долетит до середины Атлантики* (It is a rare prime-minister that can fly till the middle of the Atlantic Ocean).

This AP, using the structure of the quotation form Gogol, describes a well-known diplomatic incident between the US and Russia: on March 24, 1999, the Russian prime-minister (it was Evgeniy Primakov in those days) was flying to the US for an official visit, and having learnt that NATO started bombing Yugoslavia made a U-turn over the Atlantic ocean and went back. So the Russian folk wisdom immediately reacted to this incident by coining this phrase. The original quotation is easily recognized thanks to the same syntactic structure and partly the same wording: *Редкая/ий _____ долетит до середины _____* (It is a rare _____ that can fly till the middle of _____).

B. Relationships between Sexes

First, let us have a look at several modern anti-proverbs based on lines from popular songs.

(39)

TP: *Зачем вы, девочки, красивых любите?* (Why do you, girls, love handsome guys?) This is a line from a popular love song "Daisies Have Disappeared," lyrics by Igor Shaferan. This song, in spite of it being quite old (it was first performed in a 1971 film) remains popular and hence well-known, and it giving birth to an AP proves its popularity.

AP: *Почем вы девушки, красивых любите?* (For how much you, girls, love handsome guys?) As one can see, the meaning of the AP has nothing to do with the original romantic line, and reflects another reality of modern-day Russia: many young girls earn their living by selling their bodies. At the same time, the AP has a strong resemblance with the original saying: only one word is changed: *зачем* (why) is replaced by *почем* (for how much); these words not only rhyme, but in fact differ in two phonemes only.

(40)

TP: *Любовь нечаянно нагрянет, когда ее совсем не ждешь* (Love comes suddenly, when you do not expect it at all). Another line from another popular song "How Many Good Girls There Are," lyrics by V. Lebedev-Kumach, first performed in a 1934 film.

AP: *Любовь нечаянно нагрянет, когда жену совсем не ждешь* (Love comes suddenly, when you do not expect your wife at all). The association with the original sentence is very much the same as in the previous example: only one word is changed: *ее* (it) is replaced by *жену* (wife).

(41)

TP: *Что ты бродишь, гармонь, одиноко?* (Why do you wander, accordion, all alone?) One more line from a popular soviet song "Lonely Accordion" (lyrics by B. Mokrousov).

AP: *Что ты бродишь, гормон одинокий* (Why do you wander, hormone, all alone?) The change of meaning is quite clear, so it does not require any comments.

Much more interesting is the change in the form: only one phoneme is different in the Russian nouns *гармонь* (accordion) and *гормон* (hormone): [n'] (light n) in the original sentence is replaced by [n] (dark n) in the new version. True, the change of gender in the noun (*accordion* is feminine, *hormone* is masculine in Russian) requires the masculine gender in the modifying adjective (while in the TP *одиноко* is an adverbial modifier, which has no grammatical endings), but in the unstressed position this change, on the phonetic level, is minimal.

Now several anti-proverbs based on quotations from the poems by Alexander Pushkin (1799-1836).

(42a)

TP: *Любви все возрасты покорны* (Any age is obedient to love); that is, one can fall in love at any age. This is a line from the novel *Evgeniy Onegin*. Not every Russian will say that it is a quotation from *Evgeniy Onegin*, but every Russian will know this poem, and this phrase.

AP: *В любви все возрасты проворны* (Any age is quick in love). Quite typically, the AP has nothing to do with the original saying, but the form is nearly the same, as *покорны* (obedient) and *проворны* (quick) sound very much the same, and differ in two phonemes only, thus, they rhyme, and, besides, the syntactic structure is the same.

(42b)

AP: *Любви все плоскости покорны* (Any flat surface will do for love). Even though the form of this version is farther from the form of the original sentence, still, the structure and the rhythm are the same, and thus, the association with the original proverb is preserved, although the meaning is farther still from the original phrase.

(43)

TP: *Здравствуй, племя молодое, незнакомое!* (Greetings to the young unknown generation!) It is a line from Pushkin's poem "I Visited Again."

AP: *Здравствуй, тело молодое, незнакомое!* (Greetings to the young unknown body!) The linguistic device used here is pretty standard for this section: changing one word, and preserving the overall structure and rhythm. The meaning of the AP has nothing to do with the original quote: if Pushkin is greeting a new, younger generation, the unknown author or authors of the AP greets a new [girlfriend's] body.

Finally, several anti-proverbs based on traditional Russian proverbs and sayings.

(44)

TP: *Что посеешь, то и пожнешь* (As you sow you shall mow; similar to the English Bible proverb, *As you sow you shall reap*). Obviously, this proverb speaks not only about sowing and mowing; its figurative meaning is much broader: the consequences of one's actions depend entirely on the actions themselves.

AP: *Что посмеешь, то и пожмешь* (As you dare you shall grasp). Once again, the change of one phoneme changes the meaning completely: the figurative meaning disappears, while the literal meaning has nothing to do with the original proverb, and sounds more like a joking piece of advice. Linguistically, the AP is perfect, and has great chances to stay in the language, even if only as a wordplay: not only does it preserve the internal rhyme which is used in the TP, but also both new verbs rhyme with the verbs that they replaced: *посеешь* (sow) – *посмеешь* (dare), *пожнешь* – (mow) *пожмешь* (grasp).

(45)

TP: *Сколько лет, сколько зим!* (So many summers, so many winters!) This is a traditional greeting said when one meets somebody whom one has not seen for a long time.

AP: *Сколько Лен, сколько Зин!* (So many Lenas, so many Zinas!) Here, *Lena* and *Zina* are feminine names, the association is based on the phonetic similarity of the Russian words *лет* (summers) and *Лен* (Lenas), and *зим* (winters) and *Зин* (Zinas) respectively: these pairs differ in one phoneme only, but the result is completely different: instead of being an expression of happiness at the sight of someone whom one has not seen for a long time, the AP is an expression of happiness at the sight of many young girls.

(46)

TP: *Своя рубашка ближе к телу* (Your own shirt is closer to your body). This old Russian proverb is used only figuratively, and means that something that is your own is always more important to you than other things.

AP: *Своя Наташка ближе к телу* (Your own Natashka is closer to your body [Natashka is a girl's name]). Clearly, the figurative meaning is, once again, lost in the AP, though its literal meaning has something to do with the original saying. The standard device, used here, is rhyming words: *рубашка* (shirt) and *Наташка* (Natashka), the rest of the structure and the wording is the same: *Своя _____ ближе к телу*. The same association is used in the next example.

(47)

TP: *Не в свои сани не садись* (Do not get into someone else's sledge). Another old Russian saying, which means that one should not try to occupy a position that one does not belong to.

AP: *Не на свою Саню не ложись* (Do not lie on someone else's Sanya [Sanya is a girl's name]).

As was already mentioned, this is another example of the same association: the Russian words *сани* (sledge) and *Саню* (Sanya) sound the same; the second vowel in the unstressed final position is reduced in both words. True, unlike in #46, this example also uses the change of the verb: *садись* (get into) is replaced by *ложись* (lie), but they rhyme, and being two syllable words, preserve the overall rhythm of the sentence.

(48)

TP: *Не место красит человека, а человек место* (It is not the place that adorns the man, but the man who adorns the place). The obvious meaning is that what you are is much more important than the things that surround you or that you possess.

AP: *Не одежда красит девушку, а отсутствие оной!* (It is not the clothes that adorn the girl, but their absence!) Once again, the original meaning is lost, so in this respect this AP is nothing new. But what is new is its form. This time, the deviation from the TP is quite substantial: in fact, only the general syntactical structure and rhythm are preserved: *Не ____ красит ____, а _____* (It is not ___ that adorns ___, but ____). Still, it is enough to establish the required association, and any native speaker will recognize the original proverb behind the new version.

(49)

TP: *Любовь зла, полюбишь и козла* (Love is cruel; one can fall in love even with a goat). This proverb is similar in its meaning to the English proverb *Love is blind*: love is unpredictable, and one can fall in live with any person.

AP: *Любовь зла, уснул – и уползла* (Love is cruel: [I] fell asleep and [she] disappeared). Linguistically, a perfect coinage: it rhymes with the original saying, it preserves the same structure and rhythm, though, again, the AP lost the figurative meaning, and looks more like a joke than a folk wisdom.

(50)

TP: *Близок локоть, да не укусишь* (Close is the elbow, but [you] cannot bite it). This is an old proverb, which is used only figuratively: even though something we want may be very close it still is out of our reach.

AP: *Близок локоть, да не коленка* (Close is the elbow, but [it is] not a knee). This AP uses a language device that we have not met yet: it starts as if it were the traditional proverb (Close is the elbow, but), but then the structure changes suddenly: instead of the expected verb ([you] cannot bite it) it juxtaposes a second noun ([it is] not a knee). Thus, it defeats the expectation of the reader (hence, this device is called *defeated expectancy*), which makes the deviations still more emphatic. As a result, even though the association with the TP is preserved, the meaning changes dramatically, and instead of teaching us that something which is close at hand may still be out of reach, the new proverb tells us something much more mundane: to touch [your girl friend's knee] is much more desirable (and much more difficult) than to touch her elbow.

(51)

TP: *Нас голыми руками не возьмешь* (One cannot catch us with bare hands). This traditional Russian proverb says that it is not easy to win over (or to cheat) somebody.

AP: *Девиз холостяка: Нас голыми ногами не возьмешь* (Bachelor's motto: One cannot catch us with naked legs).

As one can see, the AP has an introductory phrase which creates the necessary context (otherwise, the meaning would be vague and in fact the AP will make little sense). With this phrase, the AP gets a new meaning: girls' legs will not make us merry. Apart from the context (bachelors), the AP differs from the TP by one word only: *руками* (hands) is replaced by *ногами* (legs): both words have three syllables; they rhyme, and belong to the same semantic field. But there is one more linguistic device that is used in this AP: the modifier *голыми* (bare) even though it appears in both TP and AP, is used in different meanings: in the traditional proverb, it means *unarmed*, while in the new proverb is has its literal meaning: *naked*. This creates an additional play on words, and hence, even though from the point of view of the form only one word is different, semantically, there are two new words in the AP: *bare arms* in the TP are replaced by *naked legs* in the AP. The moral of the new version is that confirmed bachelors know how to withstand this powerful weapon of women.

(52)

TP: *Что у трезвого на уме, то у пьяного на языке* (What the sober man thinks about, the drunken man will say). This traditional Russian proverb, which is similar to the English, *What soberness conceals, drunkenness reveals*, has a simple and clear moral: if you drink too much you lose control and may say things that should not be said.

AP: *Что у женщины на уме, то мужчине не по карману* (What the woman thinks about, the man cannot afford).

Once again, we see that the AP repeats only part of the TP, which is still enough to establish the necessary association: *Что у ____ на уме, то ____* (What the ____ thinks about, the ____). The second part, quite alien to the original saying, shows the new meaning of the AP and explains why *man* in TP is replaced by *woman* in the new version: as a rule, it is the woman who does all the shopping, and as a result, no man can afford everything that women would like to buy.

(53)

TP: *Бомбы два раза в одно место дважды не падают*
(Bombs do not fall into the same place twice). This is a traditional wisdom of the military, proven by experience. Thus, if a bomb fell near you, you can be sure that it will not fall here again.

AP: *Секс-бомбы в одну кровать дважды не падают*
(Sex-bombs do not fall into the same bed twice). This AP looks simply like a joke, but even if so, it is coined on the basis of a clear semantic association with the original saying, even though it has nothing to do with the army: it is as rare to get a sexy girl, as it is to make a bomb fall into the same spot.

C. Drinking

I will start with anti-proverbs based on biblical expressions and ancient wisdoms.

(54)

TP: *Не хлебом единым жив человек!* (Man shall not live on bread alone!) This is a well-known quotation from the Bible (e.g. Matthew 4:4). Often used in modern Russian, it has lost, in many cases, its connection with the religious context, and has acquired a broader meaning: human beings need much more for life than just food.

AP: *Не водкой единой пьян человек!* (Man shall not get drunk by vodka alone!) Once again, one should not look for any deep meaning in the AP, but thanks to its repeating the structure of the TP, it is clearly associated with it, though stating something quite obvious: there are many more ways to get drunk than drinking vodka only.

(55)

TP: *Человеку свойственно ошибаться* (To err is human).
This is a direct translation of the Latin expression *Errare humanum est*. The meaning is quite obvious: human beings are imperfect by definition, so they will make mistakes.

AP: *Человеку свойственно нажираться* (To get drunk is human). Rhyme and structure, one more time, provide the association of the AP with the TP. And one more time, there is little connection with the traditional wisdom, even though the new meaning is also wisdom, of sorts: it is really human to get drunk. It is also important to notice that the Russian verb for "to get drunk" (*нажираться*) in this case is a low colloquial word, thus making the AP stylistically quite rude.

Now, several expressions based on traditional Russian proverbs.

(56)
TP: *Кто к нам с мечом придет, тот от меча и погибнет* (He who will come to us with the sword will perish by the sword).

This is a popular quote from the soviet film, made in 1938, "Alexander Nevsky," about the Russian prince Alexander Yaroslavovich. On July 15, 1240 he defeated the Swedish army who wanted to occupy Russia. For this victory the prince got his title Nevsky (the battle took place near the Neva river). Thus, Alexander Nevsky has become a symbol of courage and patriotism; during the Second World War (on 29 July 1942) a special order of Alexander Nevsky was established. This popular quote, known to every native speaker, is, in its turn, based on the biblical expression, *Those who take up the sword shall perish by the sword* (Matthew 26:52).

AP: *Кто к нам с пивом придет, тот за водкой и побежит* (He who will come to us with beer will go to bring vodka).

Lexically, the AP is quite far from the original sentence; most importantly, it has lost the essential feature of the TP: repetition of the word *меч* (sword). Still, thanks to the overall syntactic structure, it is associated with the TP, though it has no connection with its warning to the Russian enemies. It just reflects the common life fact that many people will drink vodka with beer (cf. another popular saying, *Drinking vodka without beer is wasting your money).*

(57)
TP: *Эх, не перевелись еще на Руси богатыри – добры молодцы!* (There are still enough bogatyri [worriers] in Russia!)

38

This is a traditional pathetic exclamation found in many folklore texts, describing various events connected with defending Russia from enemies.

AP: *Эх, не перепились еще на Руси богатыри – добры молодцы!* (There are still enough sober worriers in Russia!)

Obviously, a joking play on words, but linguistically very well done: only one phoneme is changed in the original saying ([v] in the verb *перевелись* is replaced by [p] in the verb *перепились*), and the meaning is completely different, but equally true: really there are more and more people in Russia today who do not drink.

(58)

TP: *Повинную голову меч не сечет* (A guilty head will not be hit by the sword). The meaning of this traditional proverb is close to the English saying, *A fault confessed is half redressed.* Thus, if one has admitted his or her fault, one will not be punished.

AP: *Похмельную голову меч не сечет* (A drunken head [literally, *hang-overed* head] will not be hit by the sword).

One more example where the AP has very little to do with the original saying, but is still clearly associated with it: the only word which is changed is the modifier to the noun "head": *повинную* (guilty) in the TP is replaced by *похмельную* (drunken) head. Besides, and more importantly, this is not just a funny play on words: the Russian people are really, traditionally, sympathetic with the drunken compatriots, and feel pity for them.

(59)

TP: *Чему быть, того не миновать* (What is destined to happen, one cannot avoid). This is a traditional Russian proverb teaching that one cannot cheat one's destiny: what is destined to happen will happen anyway, no matter what you do (cf. a modern proverb: *If you are destined to die in an air crash, a plane will fall on your train*).

AP: *Чего пить, того не миновать* (What is to be drunk, one cannot avoid).

It is another example of nearly complete coincidence of the form: the verb *быть* (to be, here meaning *to be destin*) and *пить* (to drink) differ in one phoneme only: [b] in the first verb is replaced by [p] in the second. The rest of the structure is exactly the same, thus establishing a clear association. As for the meaning of the AP, one should not look too deep.

Now, several anti-proverbs based on famous quotations from different authors.

(60)
TP: *Бытие определяет сознание* (Being determines consciousness).

This is a well-known, in the Soviet Union times, quotation from Karl Marx (from the Preface to his work *Zur Kritik der politischen Ökonomie,* 1859); the complete sentence is: "It is not the consciousness of men which determines their existence; it is on the contrary their social existence which determines their consciousness." Even today, nearly 20 years after the collapse of the Soviet Union and communist ideology, this statement is quite often used and will be familiar to the vast majority of Russian speakers, even if they will not know the origin of this phrase.

AP: *Питие определяет сознание* (Drinking determines consciousness).

The association of this version with the original sentence is based on the same structure and phonetic similarity of the Russian words *бытие* (being) and *питие* (drinking), as they are paronyms: they differ in one phoneme only, as [b] in the TP is replaced by [p] in the AP. In fact, these two phonemes have exactly the same articulation (both are labial stops) except for one characteristic: [b] is a voiced consonant, while [p] is voiceless. Once again, even though this new saying looks like a joke, it is not, as alcohol really determines the consciousness (and thus thinking and actions) of a drunken person.

(61)
TP: *Рожденный ползать летать не может* (He who was born to crawl will not be able to fly). This is a popular quotation from the Russian writer Maxim Gorky, taken from his story "A Song about a Falcon" (1985). Its popularity is proven by the fact that, as is usual with such popular sayings, it is known to

anyone, but many people will have a hard time if one asks them about the author of this saying.

AP: *Рожденный строить не пить не может* (He who was born to build cannot but drink). This is one of the half serious, half joking commandments of college students whose major is building. It is a reflection of the fact that drinking is a part of the life of a professional builder in Russia.

(62)

TP: *Он сказал: «Поехали!» И взмахнул рукой.* (He said: Let's go! And waved his hand.) "Let's go!" is the famous phrase used by the first cosmonaut Yuri Gagarin when he was launched into space on April 12, 1961. It was later used in the popular song about Yuri Gagarin (lyrics by N. Dobronravov). And since Yuri Gagarin is known to everyone, this song (and this line) is quite popular.

AP: *Он сказал: «Поехали!» И запил водой.* (He said: Let's go! And washed it down with water.)

As one can see, only the first part *Он сказал: «Поехали!»* (He said: Let's go!) of the TP is repeated in the new version while the second is completely different: "and washed down with water." At the same time, the overall structure and rhythm are preserved, thus the necessary association with the TP is clearly established. But this is not all: the first part of the TP and the first part of the AP only look the same; the reason is that the phrase "let's go" has two meanings: (1) it can have its literal meaning, that is, one will say this phrase when one starts on a journey, or a trip, (2) it is used as a short toast while drinking; thus, "Let's go" means "Let's drink." As is usual with polysemantic words and expressions, the meaning becomes evident in the context: "And waved his hand" in the TP indicates than one is about to go on a journey. "And washed it down with water," used in the AP, clearly indicates the situation of drinking. Thus, linguistically the connection of TP and AP is multi-layered, even though there is little, if any, wisdom in the AP.

I will finish this part with an anti-proverb based on a popular commercial.

41

(63)
TP: *Спрайт – не дай себе засохнуть!* (Sprite – do not allow yourself to thirst!) This is the Russian version of the advertising slogan of Sprite "Obey your thirst."

AP: *Русская водка – не дай себе просохнуть* (Russian vodka – do not allow yourself to sober).

The AP is, of course, not promoting Russian vodka (it hardly needs any more promotion, unlike Sprite) but is simply a language joke, based on the semantic and phonetic similarity between the Russian verbs *засохнуть* (to get thirsty), used in the original slogan, and *просохнуть* (to get sober), used in the AP. It should be kept in mind that the verb *просохнуть* (to get sober), used in this sense, is a low colloquial expression. The literal (and neutral) meaning of this verb is "to get dry," the semantic relation with the meaning "to get sober" is that if you drink a lot you give yourself no time to "get dry" from the amount of alcohol you consumed.

D. Health and Medicine

I will start with an anti-proverb based on an international proverb:

(64)
TP: *Учиться никогда не поздно* (It is never too late to learn); a similar saying is found in English, French and German. The moral is clear: no one is too old to learn new things; one can learn new things at any age.

AP: *Лечиться никогда не поздно* (It is never too late to be treated [by a physician]).

This half joke, half truth is based on the phonetic similarity of the verbs *учиться* (to learn) and *лечиться* (to be treated). On the one hand, it is true that it is never too late to be treated by a doctor, on the other – it looks more like a doctor's point of view, especially today, when treatment is not cheap.

Now, several anti-proverbs based on traditional Russian proverbs.

(65)

TP: *Что с возу упало, то пропало* (What has dropped off the cart is lost). This traditional Russian proverb is similar to the English saying, *A mill cannot grind with water that is past.* In other words, what is gone is gone.

AP: *Что с возрастом упало – то пропало* (What has dropped with age is lost). This version is based on similarity, in pronunciation, of the phrase *с возу* (off the cart) and *с возрастом* (with age). Even though the second phrase has three syllables, due to it being stressed on the first syllable, (as well as the phrase from the traditional proverb) the third syllable is reduced in pronunciation, and the difference is minimal. The meaning, unlike the form, of course, is quite different. This is a perfect example of so-called black humor, physicians' slang, making fun of things that are in fact quite sad.

(66)

TP: *Горбатого могила исправит* (A person with a hump will be cured by the grave). This is similar to the English proverb, *Can the leopard change his spots?* This proverb means that as there is no cure against a hump, so one's nature cannot be changed either.

AP: *Горбатого медкомиссия исправит* (A person with a hump will be cured by medical examiners).

This is one more example of an AP reflecting modern Russian realities. There is a military draft in Russia, and all male citizens who reach the age of 18 are summoned to the recruiting office. There they are examined by special medical examiners, who check their health and whether they are able to serve in the army. It is common knowledge that this examination is very superficial, and practically speaking everyone who is summoned is found healthy enough to be drafted. Hence, the moral of this AP: even a person with a hump will be declared healthy and eligible for the draft.

Finally, anti-proverbs based on quotations from famous people:

(67)
TP: *Тяжело в учении, легко в бою* (It is difficult in training, [but] it is easy in combat). This is a well-known quotation from the famous Russian military leader Alexander Suvorov (1730-1800).[9]

AP: *Тяжело в лечении, легко в гробу* (It is difficult in treatment, [but] it is easy in the coffin). One more example of doctors' black humor that needs no lengthy explanations. The association with the TP is based on the phonetic similarity of the nouns *в учении* (in training) and *в лечении* (in treatment), and also, to a lesser extent, *в бою* (in combat) and *в гробу* (in the coffin).

(68)
TP: *Иных уж нет, а те далече* (Some are gone, and others are far away). This is a quotation from Alexander Pushkin's novel *Evgeniy Onegin*. The poet talks about his old friends, and feels sad that some of them are dead, and others are far away from him.

AP: *Иных уж нет, а тех долечат* (Some are gone, and others will be cured [till they die]). This is, again, physicians' humor: *долечат* (will be cured up to the end) in this context means that those who are still alive will die as a result of the treatment. Linguistically, the AP is very well coined, as it has the hidden rhyme with the original saying: *далече – долечат* (far away – will cure), as well as the same syntactic structure and overall rhythm, thus making the new version easily associated with the quotation.

E. Language Jokes (Wordplays)

I classify some anti-proverbs into this group because, as far as I can judge, they contain no new truth or wisdom, and are coined simply for the sake of it, as play on words. True, this aspect is present in other anti-proverbs as well, but in other types of anti-proverbs there is either a new wisdom expressed, or the old wisdom preserved. In this section, though, neither could be found, though linguistically the examples that I chose are very interesting.

I will start with anti-proverbs based on traditional Russian proverbs and beliefs.

(69)

TP: *Мусор из избы не выносить* (Do not carry your garbage out of the house). This is an interesting example of old advice which became a proverb: traditional prejudices required not to take the garbage outside, but burn it in the stove, as it was believed that an evil person could bring bad luck to the house saying some special words about the garbage. Later on, this superstition became a part of the wedding ceremony. The guests who came to the wedding tried the bride's patience by making her sweep the floor and immediately adding more garbage to the clean floor. At the same time, the guests would say, "Sweep, sweep, but not out of the house, sweep under the bench and into the stove, so that the smoke will carry it out."

Today, this old proverb has acquired a completely new figurative meaning: do not discuss your family problems in public, thus, similar to the English proverb, *Don't wash your dirty linen in public.* Incidentally, few people today will know the etymology of this TP.

AP: *Мусора, из избы не выносить* (Cops, do not carry [me] out of the house).

This joke is based on the coincidence of the two Russian words: *мусор* (garbage) in the original proverb, and *мусор* (slang for *policeman*) in the anti-proverb. But that is not all: the syntactic structure is also changed in the AP, and even though both sentences are imperative constructions, in the AP *мусора* is the address, not the object of the action *carry out.* Thus, we are dealing with a situation when police officers come to somebody's home and the drunken person says to them: cops, do not take me away (do not arrest me); leave me alone.

(70)

TP: *Не поминайте лихом!* (Don't think badly of me!) Originally, this proverb was applied only to deceased persons, as it was prohibited to think badly of them (they could retaliate). Similar beliefs are present in other languages, including, for instance, the old Latin saying, *De mortius aut bene, aut nihil*

(About the dead, either good, or nothing). Now, this expression is often used when someone is going away, so the person who is leaving asks those who stay to remember something good about him or her, and forget if he or she did something wrong.

AP: *Не поминайте лохом* (Don't think of me as a *loh*).

This joke is based on the similarity of the two words: *лихом* (literally, evil) and *лохом* (stupid person); this is modern Russian slang, mostly youth slang, and *loh* is a person who knows nothing about anything, who is easy to cheat, or deceive, or tell lies to. As we can see, only one phoneme is changed: [i] in the TP is replaced by [o] in the AP. Thus, instead of the original request not to think badly about someone, the new version asks those who stay not to think about someone as a stupid person.

(71)

TP: *Не свисти – денег не будет* (Do not whistle [in the house] – there will be no money). This is one more traditional Russian belief, based on the superstition that one can "whistle away" the money if one whistles in the house. Incidentally, even though the reason for that is lost for Russian speakers, this advice survived to this day, and any mother will tell her son today, do not whistle in the house (usually omitting the second part; thus, it is more bad manners to whistle inside than the possible reason for losing money).

AP: *Не свисти – девок не будет* (Do not whistle – there will be no girls). Of course, there is no connection whatsoever between whistling and having girls, but once again, the paronymic relationships between *денег* (money) *девок* (girls, low colloquial) establish the association between the TP and the new version. Even though the two words differ, since the stress is on the first syllable in both cases (which is the same [dc]) it is enough, and the second syllable is reduced in pronunciation.

(72a)

TP: *Одна голова хорошо, а две – лучше* (One head is good, but two are better). One more traditional Russian proverb, with a clear figurative meaning: when one has to solve some problems, two people can have more ideas than one person. Among other things, this is a good example of metonymy: we say *head* and mean *person*. This proverb gave birth to 25 (!) new proverbs, some of them repeat each other, others, in my opinion, are too silly or stupid to discuss. Let us analyze two different structures that are quite typical of the anti-proverbs based on this proverb.

AP: *Одна голова хорошо, а две головы – урод* (One head is good, but two are a monster).

Linguistically, this wordplay is quite interesting: it breaks the figurative meaning (based on metonymy) and treats the first part of the proverb (one head is good, but two are) as a literal expression, and hence, quite a logical conclusion: monster!

Another peculiarity of this AP is that it lacks the rhyme with the original expression (the Russian words *лучше* (better) and *урод* (monster) have nothing in common in their pronunciation.

(72b)
AP: *Одна голова хорошо, а с телом – лучше!* (One head is good, but with the body is better!)

Another literal reading of the original expression, but making a different and obvious conclusion: a person needs not only a head, but a body, as well. This AP is closer in its structure to the original proverb, as both the beginning and the end are the same, and the only difference happens in the middle, where *две* (two) is replaced by *с телом* (with the body).

Anti-proverbs, based on quotations from famous writers, either Russian or foreign:

(73)
TP: *Весь мир театр, а люди в нем актеры* (All the world is a stage, and people are actors). This is a famous quotation from Shakespeare, which, thanks to the popularity of his plays, has become well-established in the Russian language. The meaning is quite obvious: we all play some role or roles in life, as do actors on stage. The original quote (from the play *As You Like It*) is: "All the world's a stage, And all the men and women merely players: They have their exits and their entrances…"

AP: *Весь мир театр, а люди в нем вахтеры* (All the world is a stage, and people are door-keepers). Another joke, based on phonetic similarity of the two Russian words which have nothing in common: *актеры* (actors) and *вахтеры* (door-keepers). True, there are door-keepers in theaters, but that is as far as we can go with the meaning of the new version.

(74)

TP: *Унылая пора,* (очей очарованье!) (Melancholy time, so charming to the eye!) This is a well-known quotation from Alexander Pushkin's poem "Autumn." It is a wonderful description of the beauty of this season.

AP: *Унылая, пора* (Melancholy, [it is] time [to go]). The original saying is restructured: first, the modifier *унылая* (melancholy) has become the address in the AP: the speaker says to his girl-friend (this is marked by the feminine ending of the adjective): [my] melancholy [girl], it is time to go! Also, the second word, *пора*, though it looks the same on the surface, is different, as well: in the TP it is a noun and means "time of the year"; in the AP it is an adverb with the meaning "it is time to go." Thus, the relationships of the TP and AP are very complex, even though both consist of two words only: the form (succession of phonemes) is the same, but the syntactic structure and of course the meaning are different. One should not look for any deep meaning here, it is really just a wordplay, and a very good one, at that.

(75)

TP: *Оставь надежду всяк сюда входящий* (Leave hope anyone entering here). This is a famous quotation from Dante's *Divine Comedy*. The phrase was written over the entrance to hell, where the main hero, Petrarca, went to look for his beloved Laura. Incidentally, Alexander Pushkin uses this quote in his novel *Evgeniy Onegin* in a joking way, talking about arrogant beautiful women, who have this saying written over their foreheads.

AP: *Оставь одежду всяк сюда входящий!* (Leave clothes anyone entering here!) It is funny, and nothing else: the Russian words *надежду* (hope) and *одежду* (clothes) differ in one phoneme only: the first word has one phoneme more, the initial phoneme [n], the rest is the same.

(76)

TP: *Ничто не ценится так дорого и не обходится так дешево, как вежливость* (Nothing is valued so highly and is given to us so cheaply as politeness). This is a well-known quotation from Miguel de Cervantes Saavedra; it is often used in modern Russian.

AP: *Ничто не дается нам так дешево, как хочется* (Nothing is given to us as cheaply as we would like). This version has its own wisdom, as really, nothing comes to us free, and even if we get something cheaply we would like this something to be even cheaper, but mostly the phrase is just a joke. It is coined by omitting the first part (is valued so highly) and substituting *politeness* with *we would like*. Still, the remaining part of the original structure turns out to be enough to establish the connection with the original quotation.

The last example is based on a popular slogan, often seen in public buildings (schools, government offices, stores, etc.)

(77)

TP: *Уходя, гасите свет* (When leaving, switch off the lights). Any Russian person has seen this slogan many times and in many places.

AP: *Уходя, гасите всех* (When leaving, eliminate everyone).

Even though short, the new version uses quite complicated language means: first, it has the verb *гасить* (literally, switch off) used in the slang meaning, *to kill*. Thus, even though the first two words, from the point of view of their form, are the same both in the TP and AP, the second word (the verb) is in fact used in a different meaning, and this difference in meaning is, as usual, indicated by the context. In the original expression, the object is an inanimate thing, *light*; hence it is clear that the verb is used in its direct meaning. In the second, the object *everyone* is, of course, animate, hence, it is clear that the verb cannot be used in the literal meaning. Secondly, it uses paronymic relations between the Russian words *свет* (light) and *всех* (everyone). Even though they do differ, they both are one-syllable words, and both are stressed, and have three phonemes in common (even though their order is different): [s], [v], and [e].

Pattern III: Extension of the Traditional Proverb

This pattern also has examples in all five broad semantic groups that are used for the analysis.

A. *New Political and Economic Realities*

First, anti-proverbs based on traditional proverbs and sayings.

(78)

TP: *Всех денег не заработаешь* (One cannot earn all the money). This is an old expression, usually said to someone who is dedicating all the time to earning more and more money. It is a common sense maxim, which says: no matter how much one can earn, there will be much more money that one has not earned, while one is spending (or as many will say, wasting) life on that, depriving oneself of many other aspects of life. Thus, the moral of this saying is not that it is bad to earn money, but rather that one should not dedicate all life to that.

AP: *Всех денег не заработаешь – часть придется украсть* (One cannot earn all the money – some money will have to be stolen). As we can see, the extension gives the proverb a new meaning, and quite alien to the original one. The way to do this is standard for this pattern – the extension creates a completely new context, so the old, traditional, part acquires a new meaning, as well: now the beginning (*One cannot earn all the money*) is not a warning that there are other aspects of life which one can miss if dedicating all the time to money, but rather a justification of stealing; since it is impossible to earn money anyway, there is no other choice but steal some part of it. Thus, this AP is a great example of defeated expectancy.

(79)

TP: *Деньги не пахнут* (Money has no smell). This is a famous Latin expression, allegedly said by the Roman emperor Vespasian to his son, Tit. The son accused the father of introducing a tax on public lavatories, so the emperor made him smell the first money collected in this way, and asked him, whether it has any smell. The son had to admit that the money had no smell. Now, of course, used in a much broader sense: the origin of money is of no importance, money is money.

AP: *Деньги не пахнут, потому что их отмывают* (Money has no smell, because it is laundered). The extension, again, gives the original part a completely new meaning, and of course, is based on the play of two meanings of the verb *отмывать* (launder): (1) wash something, to make it clean and eliminate bad smell, as we wash our clothes, and (2) "make clean" in a figurative sense, that is, make clean the money acquired by illegal means.

(80)
TP: *Не свисти – денег не будет* (Do not whistle [in the house] – there will be no money). I have already discussed this proverb in the previous section (#71), while analyzing word-plays; this time, this traditional Russian belief gives birth to a modern wisdom.

AP: *И только работники ГИБДД опровергают фразу: «Не свисти – денег не будет»*. (And only traffic police refutes the phrase: "Do not whistle – there will be no money.") At first sight, this version looks like another joke, but it is not. When traffic police stops a car, they whistle. Now, in most cases they stop a car because there is some traffic violation (speeding, or some other kind of dangerous behavior on the road). This means getting a ticket, and paying a fine. Typically, many Russian drivers will try to offer money to the police, to avoid the hassle of paying the fine (one has to go to the bank to do that), and simply pay the same sum to the police officer. Hence, the double meaning of this refutation: traffic police, unlike everyone else, can in fact earn money by whistling.

(81)
TP: *Деньги – зло* (Money is evil). This is a popular phrase that emphasizes the harmful influence of money.

AP: *Наши деньги в 28,66 раза меньшее зло, чем доллары* (Our money is 28.66 times smaller evil than dollars). This phrase was recorded in 2002, when the ruble/dollar ratio was 28, 66. Today (summer 2008), this sentence would use a different ratio –

about 23 times, but that does not matter. This joke, using the allusion to the popular wisdom about the bad influence of money on people, takes it at face value and proclaims that since rubles are 28, 66 times smaller in their value than dollars, its harmfulness is 28, 66 times smaller, as well.

(82)
TP: *Поддержите отечественного производителя* (Support domestic producers). This is a popular (in any country) slogan encouraging its citizens to buy the products and services offered by the domestic companies, not foreign goods.
AP: *Девушки! Не ходите замуж за иностранца, поддержите отечественного производителя!* (Girls! Do not merry foreigners! Support domestic producers!) This version is based on the play on the two meanings of the Russian word *производитель* (producer): it can mean a company producing goods or services, and it can also mean (for instance, when talking about farms specializing in animal husbandry) a sire. When girls merry Russians, they do support "production" of more Russians, unlike the situation when they merry foreigners and consequently "produce" more foreigners.

(83)
TP: *Граждане россияне! Берегите природу!* (Citizens of Russia! Protect nature!) This is a popular slogan encouraging people to be careful about nature (not make fires in the forests, clean up garbage after themselves, etc.)
AP: *Граждане Россияне! Берегите природу родины, отдыхайте на Кипре!* (Citizens of Russia! Protect the nature of your motherland, spend vacations in Cypress!) This joke was coined by Michael Zadornov, a popular writer of short humorous stories. He uses the device that if often used in anti-proverbs: it starts as if it were the old saying, and then makes an unexpected conclusion. In this case, instead of going on to describe what one can do to protect nature (extinguish fires, pick up trash, etc.) the advice is to spend vacations (and pollute nature) somewhere else. Another great example of the defeated expectancy device: the phrase that starts as if it is a serious request ends up as a joke.

(84)

TP: *Обещанного три года ждут* (One has to wait for three years for something that has been promised). It is an old saying, with the moral that usually one has to wait a long time for something that has been promised. In other words, there is quite some time between the promise and the action.

AP: *Обещанного три года ждут. А там снова выборы* (One has to wait for three years for something that has been promised. And then it is time for new elections). This extension makes the old wisdom a very modern one (and besides, interprets it literally, while *three years* in the original phrase simply means "a long time") and applies it to a concrete political situation: elections in modern Russia. Since democratic elections are a very new thing (the so-called elections in the Soviet Union were nothing but a show[10]), it is quite easy to manipulate the people, and make them vote for the "right" candidate. The best way to do it is to promise people all kinds of good things that are impossible to implement. This is of no importance, as all that is needed is to get elected for one term; then there will be new elections, and people will be ready to believe in new populist promises.

(85)

TP: *Искусство требует жертв* (Art requires sacrifices). This is an old maxim, stating that if people choose to dedicate their life to the arts, they have to be prepared to sacrifice many things on the way; they have to be prepared to earn little money, to live in modest conditions, to save on food, etc.

AP: *Больше всего жертв требует военное искусство* (Military art requires most sacrifices). Here, we are dealing with the new context (created by the modifier *military*) that reveals new meanings of the word *sacrifices*: now it does not have a figurative meaning (lack of money, scarce food, bad living conditions, etc.), but has its literal meaning: *victims*, as it is true that military art (that is, wars) requires people to fight and be wounded or killed.

54

(86)

TP: *Где раки зимуют* (Where crayfish spend winters). This old expression is usually used in the sentence, *I will show him where crayfish spend winters.* It means, "I will teach him a lesson." Obviously, the presupposition is that the place where crayfish spend their winters is not a pleasant site.

AP: *Там, где раки только зимуют, мы живем круглый год* (Where crayfish spend only winters we live all the year round.) This is one more example of breaking the idiomatic expression (the original proverb is not about crayfish and their winters) and reinterpreting it as having a literal meaning: since it is clear that that place is not a pleasant site, the moral of the AP is that where we (Russians) live is similar to that place, but crayfish have to spend only winters there, while we live here all the time.

(87)

TP: *Дуракам закон не писан* (Fools recognize no laws). This traditional expression is used in situations when someone does a clearly foolish thing, often even detrimental to one, and thus, someone will say, *Fools recognize no laws*, meaning, what can you do with such a person?

AP: *Дуракам закон не писан. А если писан, то не читан. А если читан, то не понят. А если понят, то не так.* (Fools recognize no laws. And if they recognize them, they have not read them. And even if they have read them, they have not understood them. And if they have understood them, they understood them in the wrong way.) This is a very interesting example of stylistic development of a traditional proverb (this stylistic device is called *anadiplosis*, which is Greek for "doubling": repetition of the last prominent word of a clause in the next one, with an adjunct idea). Interestingly, it does not change the meaning much, it only emphasizes that no matter what fools do, they will never understand any commonly accepted rules of human society.

(88)

TP: *Лежачего не бьют* (One should not hit a person lying on the ground). This is a traditional rule of fair fight: two people will hit each other until one falls down, but it is unfair to keep hitting someone who is lying on the ground.

AP: *Никогда не бей лежачего: ведь он может встать* (Never hit a person lying on the ground: he may stand up). As one can see, the extension gives the original saying a completely new meaning: instead of being one of the rules of the fair fight, it becomes a warning to be careful, as the person who is lying may stand up and hit you back. Thus, this AP is another great example of defeated expectancy.

Anti-proverbs based on quotations from Russian writers:

(89)

TP: *Народ безмолвствует* (The people are silent). This is a famous quotation from Pushkin's tragedy *Boris Godunov*.[11] It describes the scene when Boris Godunov's widow and her son are poisoned, and one of the boyars announcing this news to the people says to the crowd: "Why are you silent? Shout: Long live tsar Dmitry Ivanovich!" The people are silent. Since then, this phrase (again, known to everyone, even though not many will know the exact play from which this phrase is taken) has been used to describe the situations when silent people express (by this means, silence, as the only means available to them) their disapproval of the actions of the authorities: since the people are silent instead of shouting "Long live..!" saying nothing is disapproval.

AP: *Народ безмолвствует все громче* (The people are silent louder and louder). Constructed as an oxymoron, this phrase is based on the original quote and develops its meaning: people are more and more dissatisfied with the actions of the Russian authorities, and once again, silence is their only way to express their disapproval.[12]

(90)

TP: *Какой же русский не любит быстрой езды!* (What Russian is not fond of driving fast!) This quotation is taken from the novel *Dead Souls* by the famous Russian writer Nikolay Gogol (1809-1852). One more time, this is a situation when pretty much everyone will know this phrase, even though many people may not know the name of the writer or the novel from which it is taken. This phrase is a part of the description of Russia, where Gogol compares it with the fast-going *troika* who rushes to its future, and does not answer the writer's question: "Where are you going?"

AP: *"Какой же новый русский не любит быстрой езды?" сказал гаишник, пересчитывая бабки* ("What new Russian is not fond of driving fast?" said the policeman counting the money.)

The new version is one more allusion to modern Russian mores: the so-called new Russians (or at least, many of them), who appeared after the collapse of the Soviet Union and revival of the market economy, consider themselves above the law, and so they drive without observing speed limits (besides, they drive expensive cars, and by that very fact believe that traffic rules do not apply to them). When stopped, they easily bribe traffic police, as money is no problem. Incidentally, the Russian word for money used in the AP (*бабки*) is a low colloquial word, which adds a certain stylistic flavor to the AP. It should also be pointed out that this AP follows the structure of *wellerisms* (expressions of comparison comprising a well-known quotation followed by a facetious sequel).

Anti-proverbs, based on modern sayings and realities:

(91)

TP: *Титаник напоролся на айсберг* (The Titanic was hit by an iceberg). This is a traditional explanation of the catastrophe that happened with the *Titanic* during her maiden voyage in 1912: she was going too far to the north and was hit by an iceberg, and as a result, sank on April 14th. The sinking resulted in the death of 1,517 people.

AP: *Эх, Аврора, где же был твой айсберг?* (Avrora, where was your iceberg?) *Avrora* (Aurora) is the name of the battle ship that took an active part in the socialist revolution in Saint-Petersburg in 1917. She was placed in the Neva river, close to the Winter Palace, the official residence of the Russian government. The crew supported the revolution, so when one of the ship's guns fired it was the signal for the beginning of the uprising. As we know now, this revolution marked the beginning of 75 years of the socialist experiment in Russia, which brought numerous sufferings to the peoples of Russia. Hence, the modern saying, expressing pity that *Avrora* did not meet with her own iceberg and did not sink: if it had happened, maybe the history of Russia would have been different.

B. Relationships between Sexes

Anti-proverbs based on popular sayings:

(92)
TP: *У любви свои законы* (Love has its own laws). This is a popular saying, trying to explain unpredictability of love relationships and choices (cf. #49: Love is cruel).

AP: *У любви свои законы, но чаще всего там беспредел* (Love has its own laws, but most often it has no laws at all). The extension makes the original saying more emphatic, in particular, because it uses the slang term *беспредел* (lawfulness) which originally belongs to prison slang. In modern Russian, this word is used much more often than it was originally employed, especially when describing situations (political, economic, and social) where laws do not work.

(93)
TP: *Пристал как банный лист* ([Someone] has stuck like a bath-house leaf). This popular phrase is used when one is pestered by somebody with (silly) questions, requests, etc. The origin of this saying is explained by the Russian tradition of going to public baths. Traditionally, the central part of the procedure is going to a steam-bath, where one beats oneself with birth twigs; obviously, after this procedure quite a few leaves will stick to the skin, which have to be washed off.

AP: *Мужчина как банный лист: сначала он пристает к женщине, а потом смывается* (Men are like bath-house leaves: first they stick (pester) to the women, then they wash off (disappear). The extension is based on a play on words, because both verbs (*пристает, смывается*) are used simultaneously in the direct meaning (*to stick* and *to wash off*) when referring to

58

birch leaves, and in the figurative meaning (*to pester* and *to disappear*) when referring to men.

(94)
TP: ... *на дороге не валяется* ([something or someone] does not just lie on the road). This phrase is used when talking about something or someone valuable; the moral is that you cannot get anything valuable for nothing, just walking along the road and picking it up; one has to earn that or to invest some time and effort to get that.

AP: *Хорошие мужики на дороге не валяются. Они валяются на диване* (Valuable men do not just lie on the road. They lie on the sofa). Once again, the extension utilizes the play on different meanings of the Russian verb *валяться*: it can mean *lie somewhere*, and it can mean *do nothing, be idle*. Thus, starting as if it were an example of the usage of the traditional saying (valuable men are hard to find), it continues with a completely different context, and consequently, becomes not a praise of men but their indictment.

(95)
TP: *Настоящий мужчина должен посадить дерево, построить дом и вырастить сына* (A true man must plant a tree, build a house, and raise a son). This saying reflects the traditional (patriarchal) view of the duties of the man.

AP: *Настоящая женщина должна спилить дерево, разрушить дом и вырастить дочь* (A true woman must cut the tree, demolish the house and raise a daughter). One should not look for any deep meaning or wisdom in this AP; all it does is make fun of the patriarchal mores. The wordplay is obviously based on preserving the same structure, *Настоящий/ая ____ должен/должна ____* (a true ___ must do ___), while listing opposite things: man –woman, plant a tree – cut a tree, build a house – demolish the house, raise a son – raise a daughter. Of course, to understand and appreciate the humor, one needs to know the original saying; for Russian speakers, the structure is enough to create the necessary association.

Anti-proverbs, based on quotations from Russian writers:

(96)

TP: *С милым рай и в шалаше* (With my darling, it is paradise even in the shelter made of branches). This popular saying is originally a line from the poem "In the Evening a Beautiful Girl" written by N. Ibragimov (1815). The poem became a popular song about a beautiful girl who refuses to marry a rich person and tells him that she does not need his rich mansion as it is paradise for her even in the shelter made of sticks if she has her darling with her. The obvious moral of this saying is that being with someone you love is much more important than having material possessions.

AP: *С милым рай и в шалаше, если милый атташе* (With my darling, it is paradise even in the shelter made of branches, if my darling is an attaché). This joking extension is based on the fact that the Russian words *шалаше* (shelter made of branches) and *атташе* (attaché) rhyme. Besides, it obviously refutes the old wisdom: if your darling is an attaché it goes without saying that he will have a mansion, as well.

(97)

TP: *Любви все возрасты покорны* (Any age is obedient to love, that is, one can fall in love at any age). It is a line from the novel *Evgeniy Onegin.* I have already discussed this popular quotation from Alexander Pushkin (#42), when analyzing pattern # 2. But it also gave birth to a third AP:

AP: *Любви все возрасты покорны, но только органы не все* (Any age is obedient to love, but not any organ). This extension does not make fun of the original saying, or contradict it, or in any other way ruin it, but it adds some sad but true verification to Pushkin's statement: yes, we can fall in love in any age, but not all our organs will function at a certain age. What makes this AP especially good is that it uses the same poetic rhythm as Pushkin's verse (Pushkin used iambic verse), so it reads as if it really were from his novel.

(98)

TP: *Любите книгу – источник знаний* (Love the book – the source of knowledge). This is a quotation from the famous Russian writer Maxim Gorky (1868-1936). In the soviet time, it was a standard slogan found in most public libraries and bookstores.

AP: *Любите жену – надежный источник знаний ваших недостатков* (Love the wife – the reliable source of knowledge about your shortcomings). Even though the wording and the structure of this AP are significantly changed, as compared with the original saying (in fact, what is left of it is *Love ___, the source of ___*), still it is enough to establish the connection. The meaning, obviously, has nothing to do with the original wisdom, but reflects another truth, which can be confirmed by any married man.

(99a)

TP: *Дети – цветы жизни* (Children are flowers of life). This is a famous quotation from Maxim Gorky (from his story "Former People," written in 1897). It is often used to emphasize the importance of children in the life of any person, and of the society in general. This TP gave birth to 16 anti-proverbs; all of them are based on the wordplay: *flowers* used in the literal meaning, and *flowers* meaning *children*, according to Gorky's metaphoric phrase. Since it is impossible (and there is no need) to analyze all 16 versions, I will discuss the two most interesting, and at the same time different, examples.

AP: *Дети – цветы жизни. Дарите девушкам цветы.* (Children are flowers of life. Give flowers to girls). This is just a joke, based on the play of two meanings.

(99b)

AP: *Дети – цветы жизни. На могиле родителей.* (Children are flowers of life. On the grave of the parents). Any parent will agree that it is hard work to raise a child, and the numerous problems that parents have to solve can shorten their lives.

C. Drinking

(100)

TP: *В вине мудрость* (In wine there is wisdom). This is a Russian translation of the old Latin maxim, *In vino veritas*. It is often quoted, for instance, in the poem "Stranger" by the famous Russian poet Alexander Blok (1880-1921).[13]

AP: *В вине мудрость, в пиве – сила, в воде – микробы* (In wine there is wisdom, in beer – power, in water – microbes). This joking extension, using the true fact (there are quite a few dangerous microbes in unfiltered water), twists it in such a way that it turns out that the most useful drinks are wine and beer, as they do not have any microbes!

(101)

TP: *Водка наш враг* (Vodka is our enemy). This is a popular slogan of the soviet times, advocating soberness. Incidentally, this slogan was hypocritical, as the sales of vodka have always been a huge part of the Soviet Union budget: the production was cheap, and hence the profit, based on the state monopoly, was great. Thus, the government in fact needed people to drink, while pretending to discourage them from drinking.[14]

AP: *Водка наш враг. А мы врагов не боимся.* (Vodka is our enemy. But we are not afraid of enemies.) The extension is only partly a joke; it does reflect folk wisdom: we will drink no matter what the government tells us.[15] The joke is based on the play of two meanings of the word *враг* (enemy): figurative (vodka as enemy, that is something evil and to be avoided) and literal (enemy as someone who fights against us, but we are not scared).

(102)

TP: *Алкоголь в малых дозах безвреден* (Alcohol in small doses is harmless). This is a popular medical advice that drinking in small doses does no harm to one's health.

AP: *Алкоголь в малых дозах безвреден в любом количестве* (Alcohol in small doses is harmless in any quantities). The extension, based on oxymoron (small doses – any quantities) is mostly a joke, but linguistically this is an interesting example of using the face value of some phrase, and extending it so as to make it absurd.[16]

D. Health and Medicine

(103a)

TP: *Здоровье не купишь* (One cannot buy health). This is an old Russian proverb, emphasizing the importance of good health. (There are quite a few similar proverbs). It gave birth to several AP, and I will analyze two of them:

AP: *Здоровье не купишь, хватило бы на лекарства* (One cannot buy health; you will be lucky to have enough money for prescription drugs only). This extension, in fact, develops the same idea: all you can buy (if you have enough money) is tablets and powders; health one cannot buy anyway. Among other things, this new proverb reflects a sad fact: the cost of prescription drugs in Russia today is so high that few people can afford to buy them; this is especially true about pensioners, who get miserable retirement money from the government, and more often than not this money is not enough to buy prescription drugs, which are necessary for many senior citizens.

(103b)

AP: *Здоровье уже можно купить, но еще не на что* (One can now buy health, but there is no money yet). This AP creates a different twist to the old maxim: one of the new realities of new Russia is the appearance of paid medical services. Obviously, such facilities can afford to buy modern diagnostic equipment, and to provide other modern types of treatment, which the physicians at government hospitals do not have at their disposal. Thus, the moral is, now, if one has money, one can get a high-quality medical treatment and procedures, but most people cannot afford them anyway.

(104)

TP: *Дорога ложка к обеду* (A spoon is valuable at dinner time). This old proverb teaches us that most things are valuable and important to us at a certain time; if this time is gone, they are of no value – as a spoon is very important when you eat, and of no importance when dinner is over.

AP: *Дорога к обеду ложка, а к инфаркту – неотложка* (A spoon is valuable at dinner time, and ambulance – by the heart attack time.) Using an old proverbial feature – internal rhyme (the Russian words *ложка* (spoon) and *неотложка* (ambulance) rhyme) this AP in fact confirms the old maxim, simply giving another example of a thing that is important at a certain time: it is well-known that when one has a heart attack, prompt medical help is crucial for the patient.

(105)
TP: *Необходимо вовремя обращаться к врачу* (It is necessary to visit with your doctor in time). This is a popular maxim, encouraging people to go to the doctor rather sooner than later, for obvious reasons.

AP: *Если болезнь не начать вовремя лечить – она может пройти сама* (If we do not start to treat a disease in due time it can pass itself). This joking extension uses an old stylistic device: it starts as a serious warning, as the TP, and then, when a reader expects some important medical advice, and does not expect any tricks, the AP continues with this unexpected conclusion: the disease can pass by itself. Thus, it is one more example of the defeated expectancy effect (the reader expects some serious warning about what would happen to one's health if one does not start treatment in time).

(106)
TP: *Предупреждать болезни легче, чем лечить* (To prevent a disease is easier than to treat it). This is another popular medical advice, well-known to any Russian.

AP: *Предупреждать болезни легче, чем лечить. А лечить прибыльнее, чем предупреждать.* (To prevent a disease is easier than to treat it. And to treat it is more profitable than to prevent it.) Another unexpected conclusion; it is sad but true that from a business point of view, it is better to provide an expensive treatment than a cheap preventive measure. Such inversion in the second phrase of the order followed in the first is called chiasmus. This stylistic device is used in several other anti-proverbs in my corpus.

64

(107)
TP: *Курить вредно* (Smoking is bad for your health). This is one more common sense maxim. Interestingly, the same idea is found in many old Russian proverbs, as smoking of tobacco ("Devil's substance") was condemned by strict religious mores, especially those of Russian dissenters.

AP: *Курить вредно, пить противно, а умирать здоровым – жалко* (Smoking is bad, drinking is disgusting, but dying healthy is a pity). This AP in its language mechanism is similar to the ones analyzed earlier in this section: after listing serious undisputable facts, it makes an unexpected conclusion: since everyone dies no matter whether one drinks and smokes or not, why not drink and smoke?

(108)
TP: *Богатый внутренний мир* (Rich inner world). This is a popular phrase, often used when describing people, especially when emphasizing that the true value of a person is defined by his or her inner world, not outward appearance. Cf. an English proverb, *Beauty is only skin deep.*

AP: *Хирурги считают, что внутренний мир человека лучше всего раскрывается на операционном столе* (Surgeons believe that the inner world of a person is best revealed on the operation table.) This joke is based on reinterpreting the phrase *inner world* in its literal meaning: obviously, when performing a surgery, the physicians reveal the inside of a person best of all, though of course in the original phrase by the "inner world" someone's personality is meant.

(109)
TP: *Молитва – это разговор с Богом* (Prayer is a talk with God). This is a commonly accepted understanding of what a prayer is.

AP: *Когда ты говоришь с Богом – это молитва. Когда Бог с тобой – это шизофрения.* (When you talk to God, this is a prayer. When God talks to you, this is schizophrenia.) This is another good example of chiasmus. The extension, by changing the subject and the object in the subordinate clause, makes this unexpected (though from the point of view of a psychiatrist, probably logical) conclusion. Obviously, it has nothing to do with the original saying.

(110)
TP: *Время лечит* (Time cures). This proverb is similar to the English one, *Time cures all things*. It is used in the figurative meaning, teaching us that all problems are sooner or later solved with the passing of time, and the problems that seem insurmountable today will look different in retrospect.

TP: *Время лечит, но за деньги быстрее* (Time cures, but for money it is quicker). This extension uses the popular device of reinterpreting the original proverb, and reads it literally, making its meaning refer only to medicine and cure of diseases. It is true that some illnesses will just pass by themselves even if they are not treated, but it is also true that a professional treatment will do the same quicker, though one will have to pay for that.

E. Language Jokes (Wordplays)

This section contains anti-proverbs whose main and only idea is to make fun; it is impossible to find a new moral or wisdom in these phrases, though the examples that I selected are good examples of play on words.

(111)
TP: *Вешать лапшу на уши* (To hang pasta on ears). This colloquial expression means to cheat someone, to tell lies or to promise something impossible to do. Often said about politicians running for parliament or other elected positions and promising all kinds of fantastic things, but also used in everyday context, for instance when young men try to impress young girls, they will often hang a lot of colorful pasta on their ears (according to another Russian saying, A woman loves with her ears, so this hanging of pasta works).

AP: *Если вам вешают лапшу на уши, требуйте, чтобы она была высокого качества* (If someone hangs pasta on your ears, require it to be of high quality). This play on words uses the direct meaning of the word *pasta*, hence, the joking demand that it be of high quality.

66

(112)

TP: *Враг не дремлет* (The enemy is not dozing). This is an old soviet slogan, often used in posters, encouraging the soviet people to be on the alert against possible attacks by the enemies. It should be kept in mind that the Russian verb *не дремлет* has two meanings (which is the source of humor in the AP): *not to doze* and *to be on the alert*.

AP: *Враг не дремлет – он спит* (The enemy is not dozing – he is sleeping). The source of humor is the conclusion, which goes "the other way," so to speak: a usual conclusion will be that we have to be on the alert, too; but the AP says just the opposite: the enemy is truly asleep, not just dozing. Thus, this AP is one more example of defeated expectancy effect.

(113a)

TP: *Не в деньгах счастье* (Happiness is not in money). This is a traditional saying, which, together with many similar proverbs, teaches us that money can't buy you happiness. It gave birth to several jokes which hardly need any comments, apart from the fact that they all are good examples of the play on words.

AP: *Не в деньгах счастье, а в их количестве* (Happiness is not in money, but in the amount of money).

(113b)

AP: *Верю, что не в деньгах счастье, но хочется убедиться самому* (I believe that happiness is not in money, but I would like to check it out myself).

(114)

TP: *От сумы да от тюрьмы не зарекайся* (No one can be sure that he will not be poor or get in jail). This old proverb teaches that human life is unpredictable, and no matter what one's current position in life is, one cannot be sure what will happen tomorrow.

AP: *От сумы да от тюрьмы не зарекайся, - говорит кенгуру в зоопарке* (No one can be sure that he will not be poor or get in jail, said the kangaroo in the zoo). This extension is based on the play on words: the literal Russian wording of the original proverb is: No one can say that he will not have a [beggar's] bag or get in jail. The bag, as an attribute of a beggar, is used in a metonymical sense (*pars pro toto*), but in the extension the same word means the pocket on the belly in which kangaroos keep their babies. Since the kangaroo is in a zoo, it has both the bag and is behind bars; thus, confirms the old maxim in the form of a wellerism.

(115)

TP: *Самогон ваш враг* (Samogon is your enemy). *Samogon* is home-made vodka. The slogan is one of the many soviet slogans encouraging people not to drink. We discussed the hypocrisy of such slogans earlier.

AP: *Самогон ваш враг. Гоните его!* (Samogon is your enemy. Drive it away!) The joke is based on the fact that the verb *гнать* has two meanings: *drive* somebody *away*, and *distill* alcohol. Thus, this slogan, combining both meanings, on the surface encourages people not to drink, and at the same time, to drink.

(116)

TP: *Гоняться за женщинами* (To chase women). Usually said about men who cannot miss any woman who happens to come their way (as another Russian proverbial expression describes such men, they are *chasing every skirt*).

AP: *Мужчина гоняется за женщиной, пока она его не поймает* (A man is chasing a woman until she catches him). Some will say this joke has some truth in it, but still I believe it is mostly a joke, as it juxtaposes the first clause and the second: on the surface, this is a logical contradiction, and when one realizes that, one starts looking further (or deeper) and sees the humor. This is similar to the English saying about a decent girl who never chases men: *nor does a mousetrap chase mice*.

(117)

TP: *Собака – друг человека.* (A dog is a man's friend). This is a popular (and true) description of dogs. The same proverb exists in English, *A dog is a man's best friend.*

AP: *Хорошо, когда собака – друг, но плохо, когда друг – собака* (It is good when your dog is a friend, but it is bad when your friend is a dog). The humor is lost in translation: the Russian word "dog," when applied to people, has a negative connotation. Incidentally, quite a few proverbs are based on this connotation (*A dog's death to the dog* – said about enemies or bad people, as acknowledgement of justice). Thus, it means that when your friend turns out to be a bad person, this is bad. The saying is well coined, as on the surface, thanks to the double meaning of the word *dog*, it is symmetrical, and the second part is a mirror image of the first. Thus, the AP is another good example of chiasmus used to create a new wisdom.

(118)

TP: *Старость приносит мудрость* (Old age brings wisdom). This or similar phrases contain the traditional wisdom that with age people become wiser (cf. another Russian proverb, *If the young age knew, if the old age could*).

AP: *Старость не всегда приносит мудрость. Иногда старость приходит одна* (Old age does not always bring wisdom. Sometimes old age comes alone). Once again, the joke is based on taking the verb "come" at its face value: as a person can come alone or accompanied by someone, the joke treats old age as an animate being that can come either accompanied by wisdom, or alone.

(119)

TP: *Труд сделал из обезьяны человека* (Labor has made the man out of the ape). This is a reference to a famous quotation from Friedrich Engels, often cited in the soviet time in research papers, textbooks, etc. when describing evolution of the human beings. The phrase (taken from Friedrich Engels' unfinished article *The Part Played by Labor in the Transition from Ape to Man,* 1876) emphasizes the importance of collective labor in creating a human society out of an apes' herd. Here is the exact quotation: "First labor, after it and then with it speech – these were the two most essential stimuli under the influence of which the brain of the ape gradually changed into that of man."[17]

AP: *Работа сделала из обезьяны человека, а из женщины – лошадь* (Labor has made the man out of the ape, and the horse out of the woman). The humor, as usual, is lost in translation: the second part of the AP is an allusion to the saying *to work like a horse*, which means to work a lot, do hard work and to have little or no rest. It is common knowledge that Russian women who work double shifts (one at work and the other at home) literally work like horses, hence the black humor of this saying.

(120)

TP: *Хорошо там, где нас нет* (It is good where we are not). There is a similar proverb in English, *Grass is always greener on the other side of the fence*. The moral of these proverbs is the same: we tend to believe that some other place is better than the one where we are, and usually for no reason.

AP: *Хорошо там, где нас нет. Но теперь, когда мы везде, где может быть хорошо?* (It is good where we are not. But now, when we are everywhere, where can it be good?) This is of course a joke, but incidentally reflecting a real fact: one can find immigrants from Russia anywhere in the world today, even at the most exotic places. Once again, the humor is based on the literal reading of the original proverb.

(121)

TP: *Янки, гоу хоум* (Yankee, go home). This slogan was popular after World War II and was addressed to American military forces, stationed on their bases in other countries. Since then it has been used to express general anti-American feelings (not necessary connected with US military forces) in various countries and situations. It should be pointed out that in this Russian phrase the English words are transcribed using Cyrillic letters, so it sounds, to the extent possible, as it sounds in English.

AP: *Янки, гоу хоум, и меня с собой возьмите* (Yankee, go home and take me with you). One more time we see that the humor is based on the stylistic effect of an unexpected conclusion (defeated expectancy; the mechanism of this stylistic device is analyzed in detail in section IV): the AP starts as the traditional saying, as if it condemns the US presence in other countries, but the conclusion is contrary to readers' expectation, and reflects the well-known facts that many citizens of those countries would like to go to the US if it were possible.

(122)

TP: *В России две беды: дураки и дороги* (There are two problems in Russia: fools and roads). This quotation is attributed to the famous Russian historian Nikolay Karamzin (1766-1826).[18] Since that time it has been often used and is well-known to Russian speakers today. Karamzin, of course, meant to say that Russian roads are in very bad shape, and there are too many fools in the position of authority.

AP: *В России две беды: дураки и дороги, а в Америке две радости – умники и бездорожье* (There are two problems in Russia: fools and roads, while in America there are two good things: clever people and lack of roads). The new version uses the popular trick: literal interpretation of the original phrase: as *clever people* is opposite to *fools*, so *lack of roads* is opposite to *roads* (of course, taken out of the context, while everyone understands that *roads* in the TP means impassibility of roads). Thus, the language mechanism of creating the AP is based on contextual antonymy.

Pattern IV: New Form – New Wisdom

This last pattern is different from the others: it has no direct connection to the traditional proverbs. Thus, the logical question can be asked: what is this section doing here, in the description of anti-proverbs? Are these proverbs really anti-proverbs? I hope that my analysis will provide a detailed answer to these questions; in the meantime, suffice it to say that any proverb appeared for the first time at some point as a reflection of new realities and, by that very fact, denial of old realities; in this aspect these new coinages are a class of modern anti-proverbs: in this different way they are opposed to traditional proverbs, even if they are not based on some concrete prototypes. But that is not all: even though there are no direct traditional prototypes that the new proverbs would be based on, the majority of these new coinages are based on indirect associations with historical facts and events; thus, by rejecting them or making fun of them they do, indeed, qualify as anti-proverbs even in the strict meaning of the term.

The majority of the anti-proverbs within this pattern reflect the new political and economic realities of modern Russia, some comment on relationships between sexes, and some are coined just for the sake of it, as wordplay. Since there is no direct traditional proverb with which the new proverb would be associated, I do not list traditional proverbs in this section; but in those examples where there is some hidden or indirect association with them, I will describe these, as well. Finally, I use the same five groups that were used for the two previous patterns: new political and economic realities, relationships between sexes, health and medicine, drinking, and language jokes (wordplays). As usual, some of the examples can be classified in several ways, so these groups cannot but be tentative.

A. New Political and Economic Realities

(123)
AP: *Вобла – это кит, доживший до коммунизма* (Vobla [Caspian roach] is a whale that has lived until communism). To understand the black humor of this new saying, one has to know

quite a few facts from the soviet history. First, the socialist revolution in Russia, which took place in 1917, proclaimed that a communist society, based on the ideas of Karl Marx, will be built in Russia in no time. By the late 30s the communist party stated that the basis of socialism had been built in Russia. After the Second World War the reconstruction of the country's economy was the main goal, not building communism (though it was still the big goal). In the 60s the new program of the Communist Party of the Soviet Union officially announced that "the current generation of the soviet people will live under communism." The party even gave the concrete date: 1980s. By that time, it became clear that the goal was as unreachable as ever; so the new interpretation was that the party had built the advanced stage of the socialist society, as the transitional period from socialism to communism: this stage was called *developed socialism*. It is worth mentioning that it was in the 70s and 80s that the situation with food supplies was getting worse and worse; the country depended on huge imports of grain from the US and Canada – so much for "developed socialism"! Food rationing was introduced everywhere except Moscow and Leningrad (now Saint-Petersburg).[19] Hence, a whale who will manage to live till the time of true communism will look like a vobla, if it is lucky enough to survive.

(124)

AP: *Раздельное питание – это когда народ и власть питаются отдельно* (Separate diet – this is when the people and the government eat separately). This is one more example of a proverb where the black humor is incomprehensible without the knowledge of some facts from Russian life. Throughout the soviet history, from the very first days of the soviet power, the communist party established its own system of supplies for its *nomenklatura* (top party executives). And it was not only their own food supplies in special (so called *closed*) stores, it was separate (again, closed for the general public) canteens, hospitals, resorts, summer cottages, spas, and so on, up to separate cemeteries. In fact, a member of the nomenklatura could live all his or her life without ever having to use any services that the common people (the *prols*, using Orwell's term) were using.[20]

Small wonder that they were satisfied with the political regime they had built for themselves. Incidentally, many of them could well be decent people, and were sympathizing with the difficult life that the majority of the population had, but, as another Russian saying goes, *A person who has had a big meal is not a friend* [that is, cannot understand] *to a hungry person.*

(125)

AP: *У плохого студента есть шанс стать хорошим солдатом* (A bad student has a chance to become a good soldier). This modern proverb reflects the fact of soviet and Russian life with a military draft: all male citizens who reach the age of 18 are eligible for the draft (I already discussed this problem while analyzing # 66). Students of colleges and universities get an extension, and are drafted after they graduate. Thus, many people enter colleges and universities not because they want to get a higher education, but primarily to avoid being drafted into the army. As a result, quite a few students study poorly, as they are not interested in the specialty that they have chosen (it should be kept in mind that in the Russian universities one has to choose one's major from the very start). Thus, if a student is expelled he is immediately drafted, hence the moral of the proverb: if you study poorly and get expelled you will be in the army. The words *студент* (student) and *солдат* (soldier) become contextual antonyms here.

(126)

AP: *Мы все стоим у черты бедности – правда, по разные ее стороны* (We all stand at the poverty line, but on the opposite sides of it). This is one of the many modern sayings reflecting a tremendous differentiation in the modern Russian society, as the gap between the rich and the poor is growing bigger and bigger.[21] More than that, not only the gap is increasing, but the ratio of the very rich to the poor (the vast majority of the population) is getting bigger. Hence, the black humor of this saying: the rich also can be said to live at the poverty line, though on the opposite side from the rest of us.

(127)

AP: *Социальное расслоение – это когда на одних ушах золото, а на других – лапша* (Social differentiation – it is when on some ears there is gold, on others – pasta). This saying uses the allusion to the proverbial expression *to hang pasta on ears* (I discussed it in # 111). Thus, on some ears (of the rich) one can see gold ear-rings, on the others (of the poor, that is, the majority of the population) – lies and populist promises that will never be implemented. The AP uses a popular device: play on the literal meaning of the word *pasta* and the idiomatic meaning of the same word in the expression *to hang pasta on ears*.

(128)

AP: *Если народ терпит слишком долго, его страна превращается в дом терпимости* (If the people suffer too long, their country becomes the house of sufferance). There is a play on words in the Russian text: *дом терпимости* (literary, house of sufferance) means red-light establishment. The joke is based on the cognate words: *терпеть – терпимость* (suffer – sufferance), but obviously in the phrase *house of sufferance* we are dealing with an idiom, where the meaning of the whole is not a simple sum of the meanings of its constituents. Thus, the moral of this saying is that when people suffer too long and too much, it means they are used by the ruling class in the same way as prostitutes are used.

(129)

AP: *Если бы не народ, у правительства не было бы никаких проблем* (But for the people, the government will not have any problems). It looks like a bad joke, but in fact it is not: it reflects the situation when the Russian government regularly reports about macroeconomic progress (which is most probably true) but somehow it does not tell on the lives of the ordinary people. Hence, the sad truth of this joke: the government is doing a good job of ruling the country, but somehow its people do not feel it. A similar wisdom is expressed in another modern proverb: *Стране давно уже нужен другой народ* (The country needs another people for a long time now).

(130)

AP: *После того, что правительство сделало с народом, оно обязано на нем жениться* (After what the government has done to the people, the government should merry them). The saying is based on the allusion to a situation when a man makes a girl pregnant, so the common moral law would say that he should marry her. Thus, the AP says that what the government has done to its people is against any and all moral laws.

(131)

AP: *Беда Москвы в том, что она со всех сторон окружена Россией* (The problem with Moscow is that it is surrounded by Russia from all sides). It is common knowledge that the life of any capital (or a big city) has usually little to do with the life of the rest of the country; thus, for instance, one cannot judge about the life in the US by Washington or New York. The same with Moscow. It is different from the rest of the country, and it is enough to drive a hundred kilometers (60 miles) out of Moscow to meet a vastly different way of life and level of living. Besides, Moscow has one difference from other world capitals or big cities: it is officially the most expensive city in the world[22], concentrating the majority of the country's wealth and resources. Hence, the sad truth: but for the rest of Russia Moscow itself would be fine.

(132)

AP: *Скольких товарищей потеряли мы на пути в господа!* (How many comrades have we lost on our way to misters!) This proverb is another example where one needs to know some background information to really understand the meaning. First of all, the word *товарищ* (comrade) was the usual form of address in soviet days. It was introduced as the symbol of equality of everyone (everybody is just a comrade, no sirs, misters, madams, no masters and no servants). As a result, the Russian language of the 20th century essentially lacked any form of address to an unknown man or woman. Then, after the collapse of the Soviet Union, the old forms of address were rehabilitated and slowly returned to the language: the Russian equivalents of the English words *sir, madam, ladies and gentlemen*, etc. It is only

76

natural that many people, especially the older generation, did not (and could not) accept these changes in the language, in the same way as they could not accept the changes in the political and economic life of the country, which they viewed as betrayal of the ideals of their whole lives (and in a way, it was true). Thus, we did lose quite a few people when the transition from the socialist economy and society to the free-market economy and society started.

(133)

AP: *Что у нас хорошо организовано, так это преступ-ность* (The thing that is well-organized in our country is crime). This proverb uses the allusion to the phrase *organized crime* and reflects the sad fact that organized crime has proliferated in Russia after the collapse of the Soviet Union (for instance, the flourishing or financial pyramids that literally robbed thousands of people).

(134)

AP: *Пессимист изучает китайский язык, оптимист – английский, реалист – автомат Калашникова* (Pessimists study Chinese, optimists study English, realists – a Kalashnikov machine-gun). This is an interesting example of a modern saying that reflects several contemporary realities. The first part (Pessimists study Chinese) is a reflection of the well-known fact that the Chinese comprise a large, and growing, part of the world population. The second part (optimists study English) can be interpreted in several ways, but in any event shows the dominant role of the English language in the world economy. But the most interesting is the third (and unexpected) part. Instead of giving the readers what they expect (naming some third language that would be the realists' choice) it names a Kalashnikov machine-gun. Why? Probably because in the world of growing insecurity to know how to use an AK-47 is much more useful than to know English or even Chinese.

(135)

AP: *Лучший выход из российского кризиса – Шере-метьево-2* (The best way out of the Russian crisis is Sheremetyevo-2 [international airport in Moscow]). This modern saying utilizes two meanings of the phrase *way out*: (1) solution to some problem, and (2) exit. Thus, the best way one can take to solve the problems of modern life in Russia is to leave the country.

B. Relationships between Sexes

This eternal topic is a constant source for new proverbs, and in this aspect modern Russian proverbs are no exception. Most of these example are clear, both in terms of their structure and their meaning, but some of them require brief explanations.

(136)
AP: *Счастье – иметь красивую жену, а горе – иметь такое счастье* (It is a good fortune to have a beautiful wife, and it is a misfortune to have such good fortune). The saying is based on the play of two meanings of the Russian word *горе* (misfortune) – *grief* and *problem*. Hence, the play on words is based on antonyms: *счастье – горе* (fortune – misfortune), which both refer to the same referent – beautiful wife.

(137)
AP: *Меняю рай в шалаше на ад во дворце* (I will change the paradise in the shelter of branches for the hell in the palace). This saying is based on the association with the old Russian proverb *С милым рай и в шалаше* (With my darling, it is paradise even in the shelter made of branches; I discussed it in #96). This new proverb may sound like a joke, but even if so, it has some truth to it: many people would choose material possessions as their first priority in life, especially in today's Russia.

(138)
AP: *От любви умирают редко, зато рождаются часто* (Because of love, people seldom die, but often are born). Again, there is a play on words based on different meanings of the verb *умирать* (die): used in the figurative sense (to suffer greatly), and used as an antonym to the verb *рождаться* (to be born). Indeed, people may suffer greatly when they are in love, but still

it is seldom that someone actually dies because of love; on the other hand, when people love each other they will have children together.

(139)

AP: *Свадьба – это контрольный выстрел Амура* (Wedding is the control bullet of Amor).

This short proverb requires several comments. First of all, c*ontrol bullet* is the jargon of professional killers; this is a shot in the head to make sure that the victim is dead, not just wounded. Secondly, Amor (or Cupid) is the Roman god of love, often depicted shooting his bow to inspire love, and "control bullet" in the anti-proverb is of course an allusion to this traditional description of Amor.

In other words, as a control bullet in the head makes sure the victim is dead, so the wedding ("control arrow" from Amor's bow) makes sure that the man is caught for life. This saying was probably coined by devout bachelors.

(140)

AP: *Любая юбка лучше всего смотрится на спинке сту-ла* (Any skirt looks best of all on the back of the chair). There is some distant association with women's eternal problem: what to wear and how they look in this or that piece of clothing. We can safely assume that this modern Russian saying gives men's solution to these problems.

(141)

AP: *Самый лучший способ запомнить день рождения жены – один раз его забыть* (The best way to remember your wife's birthday is to forget it once). Again, on the surface we have a logical contradiction: how can one remember by forgetting? At the same time, there is no contradiction here, because if one forgets about the wife's birthday once, there will be such a scandal that the poor husband will remember that day forever.

C. Health and Medicine

Most of these new sayings belong to doctors' slang, and depict the specific humor and views on life and death, typical for this profession.

(142)

AP: *Больному стало легче – он перестал дышать* (The patient felt better – he stopped breathing). This is one more proverb based on the stylistic effect of defeated expectancy: the first part gives the reader the idea that the patient started to recover, and so the reader expects some explanation or details of that, but all of a sudden we are told that the patient died. Of course, in a sense, when people die they do feel better (there is no more pain), but this is not that kind of improvement or cure that we normally expect from doctors.

(143)

AP: *Как врачи его ни лечили, он все равно выздоровел* (No matter how the doctors tried to treat him, the patient recovered). This is another example of the same stylistic effect: first we are told that the doctors did their best to cure the patient, but in vain; so we expect a bad end, but we are wrong, as the patient managed to survive in spite of the treatment.[23]

(144)

AP: *Больной, просыпайтесь! Пора принимать снотворное!* (Patient, wake up! It's time to take your sleeping pills!) This is just a joke, as the patient who is asleep does not need any sleeping pills, even if they were prescribed to him.

(145)

AP: *О вреде курения пишут так много, что я твердо решил бросить читать* (There are so many books about the harm of smoking that I decided to give up reading). Linguistically, this is a very well coined phrase, using the effect of defeated expectancy: up to the very end, the reader is sure that this is one more confession of a person who is convinced that smoking is damaging for health, and decided to give it up. But the last word shows that this is not the case: the person decided to give up reading, not smoking, as reading all these horror stories upsets him.

(146)

AP: *Склероз вылечить нельзя, зато о нем можно забыть* (Sclerosis cannot be cured, but one can forget about it). This is an example of one of many jokes based on this disease: since sclerosis leads to forgetting about things and people, one can forget about it, as well!

(147)

AP: *Чистая совесть свидетельствует о начале склероза* (Clear conscience means the beginning of sclerosis). There is a slight hint to the well-known maxim that everyone has sins (cf. Jesus' words, *Who of you is without sin...,* John 8:7); thus, if someone believes that he or she has a clean conscience this person probably starts to forget.

(148)

AP: *Каждая трава – лекарственная, надо только подобрать под нее болезнь* (Every herb has medicinal value; one just needs to find a corresponding disease). This saying, even if it is an exaggeration, has some truth to it: after the collapse of the Soviet Union, there was a revival of non-traditional medicine in the country; there appeared all kinds of healers using non-traditional methods of treatment, on the one hand, and non-traditional drugs, on the other. The usage of different herbs is very popular now, and if one walks into a Russian drug-store today, one really may get the idea that every herb has some medical value – so many different herbs are offered today to treat all kinds of diseases.

(149)

AP: Сами *подумайте, откуда у вас при вашем образе жизни и зарплате, могут быть хорошие анализы?* (Just think about it yourself, how can you, with your way of life and your salary, have good test results?) This saying is one more indication of both the state of medicine and of the society today. The majority of the people, who get little wages and cannot afford to buy nutritious food, on the one hand, and who have to work two or three jobs to make ends meet, on the other, of course will have health problems.

(150)

AP: *Почему так распространено отложение солей? А больше ничего отложить не удается* (Why is the deposition of salts so common today? Because this is the only thing one can deposit). This saying is similar in its moral to the previous one, and is based on the play of two meanings of the word *отложение* (deposits): as a disease (deposits of salts in the joints), and financial, as bank deposits. Since most people can hardly make both ends meet, they have no savings, of course.

D. Drinking

(151)

AP: *Встречи без галстуков позволяют больше заложить за воротник* (Meetings without ties allow putting more behind the collar). Quite a few comments are necessary to understand the meaning of the proverb. First of all, "meetings without ties" when political leaders of different countries meet in an unofficial setting (hence, without ties) were started in Russia during the presidency of Boris Yeltsin, who used to have such meetings with leaders of European countries. During these summits the leaders literally had no ties, but most importantly, they met without the official protocol, so such meetings allegedly allowed them to be more productive and better use the time of the meetings. Secondly, the Russian expression "to put behind the collar" means *to drink*. Thus, we have a play on words: when there is no tie around the collar, one can literally put more behind the collar, that is drink more. When reading this saying one has also to keep in mind that Boris Yeltsin, who did a lot for the development of democracy in Russia, had a drinking problem that was known to everyone.

(152)

AP: *Если тебя послали за пивом, значит, тебе доверяют!* (If you are sent to bring beer, it means that you are trusted!) The moral (if there is one) of this new saying is that beer is an essential component to a party; hence bringing beer is so important that it cannot be trusted to anyone.

(153)

AP: *Если вы проснулись на улице, значит, вы там заснули* (If you woke up in the street, it means you fell asleep there). This saying is another example of the defeated expectancy: it starts as a serious statement, very much like a doctor's advice or something like that (If you have these symptoms, you should do this). But the second part makes this just a joke, because the conclusion is trivial: indeed, if you wake up in the street you must have fallen asleep there!

E. Language Jokes (Wordplays)

These are just several examples of modern language jokes; they hardly require any long comments, and I give them here mostly to show that this type of modern proverbs also exists.

(154)

AP: *Пока выбьешь место под солнцем, уже вечер* (By the time you elbow your place under the sun, it is evening already). Clearly, the joke uses the play on two meanings of the phrase *place under the sun*: the usual, idiomatic meaning is to make a career, to attain some status in life; while its literal meaning is what it says: sunny place. But by the time you get your sunny place, it is evening already, so there is no sun.

(155)

AP: *Если у вас нет проблем, значит, вы уже умерли* (If you do not have any problems it means you have already died). Sounds true.

(156)

AP: *Чтобы сохранить ангельский характер, нужно дьявольское терпение* (To have angelic character one needs diabolic patience). The joke, obviously, is based on the opposition of antonyms: angelic – diabolic, but *diabolic* here is just an intensifier (very much like "awful"), thus, to be an angel one actually needs a lot of patience.

(157)

AP: *Человека хоронят два ящика – гроб и телевизор* (Humans are buried with the help of two boxes: a casket and a TV). Again, this is a play on words, because one box (casket) is actually used in the burial ceremony, while the other one (TV set) contributes to people becoming coach potatoes and thus dying earlier because of their unhealthy way of life.

3. Soviet Anti-Proverbs

While attempting to answer the most crucial question concerning modern anti-proverbs – are they short-lived coinages or are they new proverbs that will get their own place in the Russian language – it makes sense to look at similar events in the past. Obviously, any comparison is only partially valid (or, as we say in Russian, *Every comparison limps*), as every epoch has its own features and peculiarities; still, we can draw some relevant conclusions by looking at the proverbs that were created in the Russian language during the soviet period.

There are several reliable sources of the Russian proverbs of the 20th century, and I will use two of them: a collection that was published in 1957 *Пословицы и поговорки русского народа* (Proverbs and Sayings of the Russian People), which has a special section "Proverbs and Sayings of the Soviet Epoch," as well as *Словарь языка совдепии* (Dictionary of the Soviet Language) (1998) which has over 60 proverbs and sayings of the soviet period. Thus, there are about 400 examples at my disposal, which I believe is enough to offer some reliable conclusions.

These proverbs reflect three major aspects of life in the Soviet Union: soviet power and soviet motherland; defending the soviet power and motherland (these proverbs reflect the Civil war of 1918-1921 and the Great Patriotic War of 1941-1945, as part of WWII); and the heroic work of the soviet people during the peaceful times. For example:

- ***Soviet power and soviet motherland***

Была Россия царская – стала пролетарская (Russia was tsarist, now it is proletarian)
Власть советская пришла – жизнь по-новому пошла (Soviet power came – new life began)
Нет ни рабства, ни оков в стране большевиков (There is no slavery or chains in the land of Bolsheviks)[24]
За Октябрьскую нашу свободу – в огонь и в воду (For our October[25] freedom – we will go through fire and water)

Рабой жила Мария на свете, а сейчас депутат в Верховном Совете (Maria used to live as a slave, and now she is a deputy in the Supreme Soviet[26])

Жена мужу подруга, а не прислуга (The wife is her husband's friend, not a servant)

Была коптилка и свеча, теперь – лампа Ильича (There used to be only wick lights and candles, and now we have Ilyich's[27] lamp)

Без бога шире дорога (Without God the road is wider)

Грянул гром – бегу в райком, нету грома – бегу мимо райкома (If there is thunder, I run to the regional committee[28], if there is no thunder – I pass by the committee)

Красно поле снопами, а Советская власть делами (The field is made beautiful by its sheaves, and the soviet power – by its deeds)

- ***Defending the soviet power and motherland***

Конница Буденного бьет врага пешего и конного (The cavalry of Budenny[29] attacks the enemy both on foot and on horseback).

У генералов длинные ноги, да не нашли к Москве дороги (Generals have long legs, but still could not find a way to Moscow).

Красный Питер бока Юденичу вытер (Red Piter[30] beat Yudenich[31]).

Белые так удирали, что у них сапоги с ног слетали (The white army was running away so quickly that their boots fell off their feet).

Наша грозная сила – фашистам могила (Our strong power is the grave for fascists).

Советский боец и один в поле воин (A soviet soldier can even fight alone)

Фашисты нам яму рыли, да сами в нее угодили (The fascists were digging a hole for us, but got there themselves)

- ***Heroic work of the soviet people during the peaceful times***

Любишь премироваться, люби и план перевыполнять (If you like to get bonuses, you have to like to do more than was planned)

Колхозник колхозника по работе узнает (A member of a collective farm recognizes another member by his work)

Рапортовать не спеши: план выполни, тогда рапорт держи (Do not hurry to report: first fulfill your plan, then report)

Хлеб дает нам не Христос, а машина и колхоз (Bread is given to us not by Christ, but by machines and collective farms)

Набирайся силы у груди матери, а ума у коммунистической партии (Get strength with you mother's milk, and get wisdom from the communist party)

Без хорошего труда нет плода (There is no fruit without good work)

Час смену бережет (An hour takes care of the whole shift)

Колхоз пашет, а лодырь руками машет (A collective farm is sowing, and a lazy person is waving his hands)

Недаром говорится – кулак колхоза боится (It is really true: the kulaks[32] are afraid of collective farms)

Хорошая нива только у коллектива (A good harvest is had only by a collective farm)

В колхозную пору пошла жизнь в гору (During the collective farm era, our life got better).

В колхоз войдешь – богато заживешь (If you join the collective farm you will prosper).

As one can see, the most characteristic feature of these and many other soviet proverbs is that they all are based on rejection and criticism of the old ways of life, be that old land ownership, or family relationships, or religion – all these things were considered unacceptable any more, and were rejected as something alien, and not needed for the soviet people. They did not need their individual land plot – they had collective farms now, where they worked together and the results were better, and they were more well-to-do than before the revolution. They did not need any tsar or God – they had the communist party now that would tell them exactly what to believe in, and what not to believe in.

They did not have to rely on God's help any more – again, communists would take care of them now, and so on. There was hardly any aspect of pre-revolutionary life that was left unchanged by the leaders of new Russia.

At the same time, in terms of form, the vast majority of these new proverbs are coined using one of the most traditional proverbial patterns in the Russian language – short rhythmical sentences with internal rhyme. Thus, they are easy to pronounce and easy to remember; they do look as any traditional Russian proverb. But did they become real proverbs themselves?

To be able to draw some valid conclusions, we now need to have a closer look at the soviet proverbs using the same four major patterns that were used for modern Russian AP:

1. *Similar form - same wisdom*
2. *Similar from – new wisdom*
3. *Extension of the traditional proverb*
4. *New form – new wisdom*

Similar Form – Same Wisdom

There are very few examples of soviet proverbs that would use this pattern among the 400 examples that I have.

Любишь премироваться, люби и план перевыполнять (If you like to get bonuses, you have to like to do more than was planned).

This proverb clearly follows the structure of the traditional Russian proverb *Любишь кататься, люби и саночки возить* (If you like to ride the sledge you should like to push it, as well.) The figurative meaning of the traditional proverb is obvious, and quite common for Russian folk wisdom: if you like to play, you should like to work (similar to English, *All work and no play makes Jack a dull boy*). The soviet version clearly repeats the traditional moral, but at the same time makes it more narrow and applicable to the new realities only: it emphasizes over-fulfilling the amount of work as the precondition of getting a bonus. Obviously, the figurative (or to be more exact, generic) meaning is lost – and this is another common feature of soviet proverbs:

they inevitably lose the figurative meanings (or never had one) and are used only in the narrow and quite literal sense; thus, this one talks only about doing more than was planned, and nothing else.

Рапортовать не спеши: план выполни, тогда рапорт держи (Do not hurry to report: first fulfill your plan, then report).

This proverb loosely follows the structure of another traditional Russian one: *Не говори гоп, пока не перепрыгнешь* (Do not say "gop"[done] until you jump over [something]). (This proverb is the prototype of a modern Russian AP, as well, which was analyzed earlier, see #11). The proverb is used only metaphorically, and means, obviously, that one should not boast about doing something until he or she has actually done it. It is similar to the English saying, *There is many a slip between the cup and the lip.*

Once again we see the same change here: the proverb loses its figurative meaning completely, and now refers to only one concrete situation: work, even though it means basically the same: first do your work then report about having done it.

Фашисты нам яму рыли, да сами в нее угодили (The fascists were digging a hole for us, but got there themselves).

This proverb is based on the traditional Russian proverb *Не рой другому яму, сам в нее попадешь* (Do not dig a hole for another person – you will get into it yourself). The original proverb is taken from the Bible: *He who digs a hole and scoops it out falls into the pit he has made* (Psalms 7:15). One more time, it is used only figuratively and warns people not to do bad things towards others, as the evil you have done will return back to you.

And again, the soviet version narrows the meaning to a concrete situation of the Second World War: fascists were trying to harm us, but they harmed themselves. Figurative meaning, even though present in the idiom "to dig a whole" is basically lost, as this version, unlike the traditional proverb, cannot be applied to any other situation.

Similar Form – New Wisdom

For this pattern, the situation is the opposite one: many soviet proverbs follow it.

Красно поле снопами, а Советская власть делами (The field is beautiful by its sheaves, and the soviet power – by its deeds).
This is clearly a new version of the traditional Russian proverb *Не красна изба углами, а красна пирогами* (The house is beautiful not by its corners, but by its pies), which means, roughly, when you visit someone, the food you are treated to is more important and tells you more about the hostess than the appearance of the house). The new version, as well as the TP, has internal rhyme: *снопами* (sheaves) and *делами* (deeds) rhyme, (as well as *углами* (corners) and *пирогами* (pies). So though the meaning of the AP has nothing in common with the TP, it uses its syntactical and phonetic structure, thus making it easier to accept and remember.

Советский боец и один в поле воин (A soviet soldier can even fight alone).
This is an AP version of the traditional proverb *Один в поле не воин* (One person cannot fight [an army]). The soviet proverb not only has a different (in fact, opposite) meaning, but it clearly denies the old wisdom: it was in old days that one could not fight alone, now, the soviet people can fight even if it is only one person against an enemy army.

*Колхозник колхозника по работе узнает (*A member of a collective farm recognizes another member by his work).
This proverb repeats the structure of the traditional Russian proverb, *Рыбак рыбака видит издалека* (literally, a Fisherman sees another fisherman from afar). The traditional proverb is used only figuratively and has the same meaning as the English saying *It takes one to know one*: people who have similar interests recognize each other. The traditional proverb, typically, has internal rhyme.

The soviet version, one more time, narrows the meaning to a concrete situation, and now refers to only collective farm members, who allegedly recognize each other by their (good) work; hence, it cannot be used figuratively. Linguistically, it is inferior to the TP, as there is no internal rhyme here.

Час смену бережет (An hour takes care of the whole shift).

This soviet proverb is built on the basis of the traditional phrase *Копейка рубль бережет* (A kopeck [one-hundredth of a ruble] takes care of the ruble). The traditional proverb has the same meaning as the English *Take care of the pence and the pounds will take care of themselves*.

And again, we see that the soviet version, even though following the same structure (and thus, clearly being associated with the TP), changes the meaning completely, and now warns the soviet people not to waste time when working. Incidentally, the AP loses the rhythm of the traditional proverb, and thus is more difficult to pronounce than the TP.

Extension of the Traditional Proverb

Extensions of traditional Russian proverbs are rare; in fact, I could find only two examples of this pattern:

Набирайся силы у груди матери, а ума у коммунистической партии (Get strength with you mother's milk, and get wisdom from the communist party).

There is a traditional Russian phrase, *всосать с молоком матери* (literally, to suck with the mother's milk) which means that it is at an early age when it is determined what this person will be when he or she grows up.

The new version, as one can see, does not stop here, and – one more time – makes the meaning concrete: get strength with your mother's milk, but get wisdom from the communist party (obviously, because now one cannot become wise without the guidance of the communists). Linguistically, the new version follows the traditional pattern, as it preserves the internal rhyme which is so common in Russian folk wisdom.

Грянул гром – бегу в райком, нету грома – бегу мимо райкома (If there is thunder, I run to the regional committee [of the communist party], if there is no thunder – I pass by the committee).

This is an extension of the traditional Russian saying, *Пока гром не грянет, мужик не перекрестится* (literally, a Russian will cross himself only when he hears thunder). This proverb has only a figurative meaning: it is typical for a Russian person to procrastinate till the very last moment until he would take some measures to deal with the problem.

Of course, the new version could not have anything to do with religion (even though, again, "to cross" in the original phrase is used figuratively – to do something), and instead suggested the new authority – the communist party. So, interestingly, it is criticizing people for being inactive (and in this aspect, repeats the traditional proverb), but of course mentions the communist party as the place where even such people will find help.

New Form – New Wisdom

This is by far the largest groups of soviet proverbs:

Хлеб дает нам не Христос, а машина и колхоз (Bread is given to us not by Christ, but by machines and collective farms).

Many new soviet proverbs, even though they have no connection, either in form or in meaning, with the traditional Russian proverb, still preserve some allusion to well-known quotations. Thus, this one is clearly associated with the story about five loaves of bread and two fishes that Christ used to feed 5,000 people (John 6:11). But this association is used not to give more authority to a new saying, but to deny the old wisdom: now soviet people do not need any miracles to feed them, as they have collective farms and new machines which guarantee them a lot of bread.[33]

Linguistically, though, this AP is very good, as it copies both the rhythm and the rhyme of traditional Russian proverbs. At the same time, as was mentioned for the previous examples, this AP has no figurative meaning and can be used only literally.

Недаром говорится – кулак колхоза боится (It is really true: the kulaks are afraid of collective farms).

This AP is one more propaganda phrase about collective farms, the idea being that individual land owners are allegedly afraid of collective farms because they cannot compete with them.[34]

The proverb has internal rhyme, so it looks like any traditional Russian proverb, though, again, it has no meaning outside its literal usage. It is loosely associated with the Russian proverb *Дело мастера боится* (literally, The work is afraid of the master), which means that no work or task is too difficult if you know how to do it. There is hardly any semantic connection between the TP and the AP, though.

Here are some more examples of new soviet proverbs; all of them proclaim some new positive features of the soviet Russia, as compared with the old pre-revolutionary times; they all use internal rhyme and rhythm, and hardly need any comments regarding their meaning, as they completely lack any figurative meaning:

Была Россия царская – стала пролетарская (Russia was tsarist, now it is proletarian)
Власть советская пришла – жизнь по-новому пошла (Soviet power came – new life began)
Без бога шире дорога (Without God the road is wider)
Нет ни рабства, ни оков в стране большевиков (There is no slavery or chains in the land of Bolsheviks).

Thus, the majority of the soviet proverbs belong to the last pattern – new form – new wisdom (although, as I have already said, they do follow the general rhythmical and rhyming models of traditional Russian proverbs and saying). Isn't that one of the main reasons why they did not stay? It seems logical to suggest that since there was a semantic gap (no doubt, deliberate – to show that new wisdom has nothing to do with old prerevolutionary life) between the soviet proverbs and traditional Russian proverbs, there was also no semantic connection between them (confirming old wisdoms by new forms, or new choice of words, or new realities), and thus, they were doomed to extinction as soon as the society changed. Such result was only natural: since these proverbs had no figurative meaning, they could not be applied to any other situation except the one that they were coined for; once those situations or realities were gone, they immediately became "unemployed," as they now reflected nothing. Let me repeat: this is a key difference of these proverbs and traditional Russian proverbs: even though the realities that gave birth to traditional Russian proverbs are long gone, thanks to their figurative meaning they continue to be used, as they are not so rigidly connected with those realities. Let me give you an example from Russian history.

There is a traditional Russian proverb *Как Мамай воевал* (literally, as if Mamay was fighting here). It refers to an important historical event in Russian history – the occupation of Russia in the 13-15th centuries by Tatars; Khan Mamay being one of the military leaders of the Tatars in the 14th century. This occupation is known for a lot of suffering and destruction brought by the aggressors. And since it was such a major event, the collective memory of the Russian people preserved the recollections of that dark period in Russian history by means of numerous proverbs, all of them use the references to Tatars as something evil and alien, for example, *Незваный гость хуже татарина* (Unexpected guests are worse than Tatars), *Мамаево побоище* (Mamay battlefield), and so on.

Now, the realities that gave birth to this proverb do not exist any more, still, it survived due to its figurative meaning: complete mess, disorder, devastation. For example, it is often used by parents who see the mess in the room of their children.

So, what has happened to the soviet proverbs? To check whether any of them survived one needs to analyze a modern collection of Russian proverbs to see if any of those proverbs are recorded in the collections of the early 21st century.

For this analysis I took three of the latest collections of Russian proverbs issued in 2005- 2007:

K.G. Bersenyeva. *Russkiye poslovitsy i pogovorki* (Russian proverbs and Sayings). Moscow, 2005. 383 pages. The number of proverbs and sayings included in the dictionary is not mentioned; but judging by the size one of the book one can safely assume that there are at least 1,000 proverbs and sayings.

V.I. Zimin, A.S. Spirin. *Poslovitsy I pogovorki russkogo naroda* (Proverbs and Sayings of the Russian People). Moscow, 2006. 537 pages. This dictionary is an outstanding work of lexicography: it contains about 40,000 (yes, forty *thousand*) proverbs and sayings and is the result of 35 years of collecting them all over Russia.

V.M. Mokienko et al. *Slovar russkih poslovits* (Dictionary of Russian Proverbs). Moscow, 2007. This dictionary contains over 1,000 proverbs.

The analysis was easy to do: none of the 390 proverbs is listed in any of these collections. And it is not surprising: the soviet anti-proverbs, even though they were constructed according to all the language rules and are linguistically perfect, did not stay in the language, partly because they were artificially imposed and never really became folk wisdom, and partly because there was a deliberate semantic gap in their meaning as compared to the meaning of traditional Russian proverbs. Lastly, the soviet proverbs completely lacked any figurative meaning. Thus, ironically, it is really true (this is one more soviet proverb) that *Старая пословица с новым веком ссорится* (Old proverbs quarrel with the new era).

But maybe these new dictionaries have no proverbs of the soviet period because of the new political situation? In other words, maybe they ignore the soviet proverbs and sayings not because they do not exist any more, but because it is politically incorrect to mention them today, as it is incorrect to mention many other attributes of the soviet epoch?

To check that assumption, I took two dictionaries issued in the 80s and early 90s when there was hardly any bias against the soviet realities:

V.P. Felitsina, Yu. E Prokhorov. *Russkiye poslovitsy, pogovorki i krylatye vyrazheniya* (Russian Proverbs, Sayings and Famous Quotations). 2nd ed. Moscow, 1988. 272 pages. The dictionary contains 450 proverbs and sayings.

V.P. Zhukov. *Slovar russkih poslovits i pogovorok* (Dictionary of Russian Proverbs and Sayings). 5th ed. Moscow, 1993. The dictionary contains over 1,000 proverbs.

The result was the same: none of the 390 soviet proverbs that are at my disposal are listed in these two dictionaries.

Does this mean that the modern Russian anti-proverbs will disappear as their soviet predecessors did? Obviously, it is too early to judge, but the analysis of the soviet proverbs allows us to tentatively suggest that modern anti-proverbs, at least some of them, will definitely stay. They do not exhibit such a deliberate and abrupt semantic gap between themselves and the traditional Russian proverbs as the soviet coinages had; as we have seen, quite a few of them reiterate old wisdom using new forms or new realities; some of them are based on well-known slogans or quotations; those of them that do reflect new wisdom do so not because someone imposed them from above, but are really the product of folk creativity and for that reason alone have better chances of survival. Besides, quite a few of modern anti-proverbs have acquired proverbial (figurative) status already, so we can safely assume that they will stay.

4. Language Mechanisms Used in Creating Anti-Proverbs

It is now time to look at the modern Russian anti-proverbs from a different angle and try to analyze and classify the language mechanisms that are used in creating them. Many of these devices were mentioned while examining various types of anti-proverbs, but the overall picture of the ways by means of which anti-proverbs are created would be lost if I did not sum up these observations in a special section.

The corpus of my examples shows that the range of mechanisms by means of which modern Russian anti-proverbs are formed (and related to their prototypes, when they have them) is quite wide; these mechanisms belong to all language levels, from phonetic to syntactic, though of course some of them are more common and some of them are used only occasionally. Besides, some of the mechanisms are difficult to classify as belonging to a certain level, so I will discuss them separately.

1. Phonetic mechanisms:
   - homonymy
   - paronymy
   - internal rhyme
   - hidden rhyme (rhyming substitution)

2. Morphological mechanisms:
   - spoonerism
   - English words with Russian morphological endings
   - neologisms

3. Lexical mechanisms:
   - polysemy
   - antonymy
   - synonymy
   - new lexical content of the same syntactic structure

4. Syntactic mechanisms:
   • restructuring
   • extension

5. Stylistic mechanisms:
   • metaphor
   • metonymy
   • oxymoron
   • chiasmus
   • anadiplosis
   • wellerism

6. Defeated expectancy

7. Combination of different mechanisms

While explaining and exemplifying various language means I will try to use new examples that were not analyzed in the previous chapters, with the exception of those mechanisms that are rarely used.

Phonetic mechanisms:

- homonymy
- paronymy
- internal rhyme
- hidden rhyme (rhyming substitution)

Homonymy

Homonyms are words that sound and/or look alike but have nothing in common from the point of view of their meaning.

This traditional linguistic device, somewhat surprisingly, turned out to be quite rarely used in the formation of modern Russian anti-proverbs. Still, my corpus contains a couple of interesting examples:

AP: *Если народу все по барабану, то государству – труба* (literally, If everything is to drums for the people, then it is trumpet to the state). The literal meaning of the phrase makes no sense, because there are two idioms in it; at the same time, the sad joke is based on the homophonic relationships between the Russian words *барабан* (drums) and *труба* (trumpet) when they mean musical instruments, on the one hand, and when they are used in idioms in a completely different meaning which has nothing to do with music – on the other. So in fact linguistically this is a very interesting example of multi-level meaning. Let us try to make some sense of it.

The Russian idiom *все по барабану* (everything to the drums) means one could not care less about something. The Russian idiom *труба (кому-либо)* (trumpet to somebody) means that the situation is very bad for somebody. Thus, the AP means: if the people are indifferent to what is going on then the country is in a bad situation. But it sounds much better and much more interesting in Russian because the homophonic words *барабан$_1$* (drums) and *барабан$_2$* (as part of the idiom), as well as *труба$_1$* (trumpet) and *труба$_2$* (as part of the idiom) create a play on words based on the literal meaning of these words, as both of them name a musical instrument.

A similar device is used in the following anti-proverb that was analyzed already (#14):

TP: *Не переходите улицу на красный свет* (Do not cross the street when the light is red). This, in fact, is not so much a proverb as a well-known saying (traffic rule), one of those basic things that kids are taught in school, hence, well-known to everyone.

AP: *Не переходите улицу на тот свет* (Do not cross the street to the other world). That is, if you cross the street when the light is red, you will get hit by the car and die.

The peculiarity and black humor of the AP is based on the play on words: the Russian words *light* and *world* are homonyms; hence, literally, (красный) *свет* (red) *light* and (тот) *свет* (the other) *world* sound and look the same.

Paronymy

Paronyms are words that sound alike, though they may have no semantic connection. There is a fine line between paronyms and homonyms, but still homonyms sound exactly the same, while the paronyms sound similar but are still different. This way of the formation of anti-proverbs is quite common:

TP: *Не отрекаются любя* ([Those who] love do not denounce [their love].

AP: *Не отвлекаются любя* ([Those who] love do not divert [their attention]).

This AP clearly belongs to language jokes, so in terms of meaning is not too interesting, but the formation is typical: it takes a line form a very popular song by the famous Russian singer Alla Pugacheva, changes one phoneme ([r] to [l] – both of them belong to the same group of so-called liquid consonants, and their articulation is very similar) and makes it a joke.

One more example:

TP: *Голь на выдумки хитра* (The poor are creative).

AP: *Голая на выдумки хитра* (The naked [girl] is creative).

The traditional proverb is an old and popular saying which means that the poor people have to be creative and find ways to survive; in a way, it is similar to the English saying, *Necessity is the mother of invention.* The AP of course is a joke, based on the similar sounding of the (old Russian) noun *голь* (the poor) which has a feminine gender in Russian, and the adjective *голая* (*naked* in the feminine gender, that is, a naked girl).

Internal rhyme

One of the typical elements of traditional Russian proverbs and sayings is internal rhyme, which, combined with a distinct rhythm, makes them easy to pronounce and remember. In this aspect, anti-proverbs are as conservative as they can be, as the vast majority of them also have a clear rhythm and internal rhyme. This element of anti-proverbs was mentioned many times (see, for example, ## 7, 25, 28, 49, 96), but I can add a couple of new examples that were not discussed.

TP: *Кто рано встает, тому бог подает* (He who gets up early is helped by God).

AP: *Кто рано встает, с тем бог поддает* (He who gets up early, drinks with God).

The original proverb expresses a common wisdom that people who get up early manage to do more and hence, they can say that God is on their side (literally, God gives them). The AP using similarity of the form of the verbs *подает* (give) and *поддает* (drink, in low colloquial style) makes it a wordplay.

Both the original proverb and the new version have internal rhyme: *встает – подает* (gets up – helped), *встает – поддает* (gets up – drinks), so the AP follows its prototype very closely.

AP: *Любовь начинается идеалом, а кончается одеялом* (Love starts with an ideal and ends with a blanket). This is an original AP that has no traditional prototype, and in terms of meaning presents an old wisdom: any romantic relationship sooner or later ends in a bed. For this analysis, it is much more interesting in its form: even though it has no traditional prototype, it utilizes a traditional device of internal rhyme: *идеалом – одеялом* (the Russian words *ideal* and *blanket* rhyme in instrumental case).

Hidden rhyme (rhyming substitution)

This is by far the most interesting linguistic feature of modern Russian anti-proverbs, even though it is not unique to these coinages. In fact, this very commonality is a key to understanding many aspects of the AP phenomenon.

By internal rhyme I mean that many modern Russian anti-proverbs use the so-called rhyming substitution, that is, they rhyme with the traditional proverb that was used as their pattern or prototype. The rhyme is hidden, because in the resulting AP there is no rhyme per se, and in order to understand it one needs to know (and to recognize) the traditional proverb in its AP version. For example:

AP: *Из всех искусств для нас важнейшим является вино* (Of all the arts the most important for us is wine).

This language joke is based on the well-known (at least, well-known to the people who lived in the soviet era) quotation from Vladimir Lenin:

TP: *Из всех искусств для нас важнейшим является кино* (Of all the arts the most important for us is cinema). Lenin paid much attention to this new form of mass propaganda, because he understood its possibilities, hence this famous quotation.

The AP is of course just a joke, but in order to understand the humor (otherwise, it makes little sense – why wine is a form of art?) one has to recognize the prototype sentence, and to help the reader in this the AP has the hidden rhyme, as the Russian words *cinema* and *wine* (*вино – кино*) rhyme.

The same device is used in quite a few modern Russian anti-proverbs that were analyzed earlier (#68):

TP: *Иных уж нет, а те далече* (Some are gone, and others are far away). This is a quotation from Alexander Pushkin's novel *Evgeniy Onegin*. The poet talks about his old friends, and feels sad that some of them are dead, and others are far away from him.

AP: *Иных уж нет, а тех долечат* (Some are gone, and other will be cured [till they die]). This is physicians' humor: *долечат* (will be cured up to the end) in this context means that those who are still alive will die as a result of the treatment.

Once again, to fully understand the humor of the new coinage one needs to recognize the underlying quotation from Pushkin; and to help the reader see the connection, the AP has a (very well made) hidden rhyme: *далече* (far away) in the original sentence rhymes with *долечат* (will be cured up to the end) in the new version.

One more example of the same mechanism used in a modern anti-proverb based on a quotation from another Russian poet (#31):

TP: *И скучно, и грустно, и некому руку подать* (I am bored, and sad, and have no one to shake hands with). This is the first line from a well-known poem of the great Russian poet Michael Lermontov (1814-1841), describing his loneliness in the Russian society of his days.

AP: *И скучно, и грустно, и некому тело продать* (I am bored, and sad, and have no one to sell my body to). The meaning of the AP has nothing to do with the original saying, although it does repeat its structure and rhymes with the TP: the verbs *подать* (shake) and *продать* (sell) not only rhyme, but in fact differ only in one phoneme: the latter one has one more phoneme, phoneme [r].

As I have already said, this interesting feature, even though it is essential to the understanding of AP phenomenon, is not unique to modern Russian APs; for example, it was the standard device used by London cockney slang, which in its own way, was also a folk creation.

Just to remind the readers who may be unfamiliar with this social dialect of London of the early 20th century. In cockney, every word or phrase rhymes with the noun it substitutes, but since the substituted word is not pronounced (that was the main idea – to make it impossible for outsiders to understand) the rhyme is hidden. For example:

Eyes in cockney are *mince pies*. So if one said, *She has lovely minces*, only the initiated could understand that what was meant was that she has lovely eyes.
Head is a *crust of bread*. So, in a sentence, *Use your crust* one is advised to think.
Wife is *trouble and strife*. Hence, *It is only me and trouble at home* means "me and my wife."
Dustbin lids means kids, and so on.[35]

Thus, this comparison leads to a very interesting and important conclusion. Hidden rhyme seems to be not only one of the key linguistic features of modern Russian APs, but it is probably a key feature of folk coinages irrespective of the language: London cockney and modern Russian anti-proverbs, as well as the English and Russian languages in general, have little in common, so hidden rhyme is clearly common not because of the common structure but because of the common register: both cockney rhyming slang and modern Russian APs are folk creations, and in both cases one needs to know the substituted word or phrase from the standard English or Russian to be able not only to understand the meaning but also (and maybe more importantly) appreciate the folk humor and folk wisdom.

Morphological mechanisms:

- spoonerisms
- English words with Russian morphological endings
- neologisms

Spoonerisms

Spoonerisms (the term comes from the name of the Oxford professor William A. Spooner, 1844-1930) are words or phrases in which letters or syllables get swapped, thus creating humorous effect. A lot of such coinages are attributed to Spooner, for example, "The weight of rages will press hard upon the employer."

Spoonerisms are rare, at least, in the material that I have at my disposal. There is only one example of this stylistic device, though it is a very good one:

TP: *Крепче за баранку держись, шофер!* (Hold tighter the steering wheel, driver!)

AP: *Крепче за шоферку держись, баран!* (Hold tighter the [girl] driver, ram!)

One more time, the literal translation means nothing, because there are quite a few levels of play on words here.

Let us start with the TP. It is a line from a very popular soviet song (lyrics by G. Nikitinsky) about a driver of a truck who is driving along a road and thinks about his girlfriend who waits for him at home; so the refrain warns him: so that your girl friend will not have to cry, hold tighter the steering wheel! The Russian word used for *steering wheel* is a colloquial expression which is taken from professional drivers' lingo: *баранка* literally means bagel (ring-shaped roll) and is used to name a steering wheel because of the similar form.

But the root of this word coincides with the Russian word *баран* (ram), though these two words have nothing in common etymologically. Thus, when the AP changes the places of *steering wheel* and *driver*, we get a completely new phrase: here, the word *шоферка* (feminine driver) acquires a feminine suffix, left here from the word *баранка* (steering wheel) in the original sentence, and the word *баранка*, left without its suffix and feminine inflexion, now becomes the Russian word *баран* (ram). When applied to people, it is similar to English *moron*; in other words, it is a joking piece of advice for a shy boyfriend: hold tighter the girl who is driving!

English words with Russian morphological endings

This device is rare, as well; I have only one example that was discussed earlier (#15):

TP: *Чем бы дитя ни тешилось, лишь бы не плакало* (Whatever the child plays with, the most important thing is that it does not cry). Thus, anything is worth allowing the child to do as long as it does not cry. Figuratively (and often ironically) said about adults who do something unusual or strange for a grown-up person, but like it anyway.

AP: *Чем бы дитя ни тешилось, лишь бы не факалось* (Whatever the child plays with, most important is that it does not fuck).

The Russian saying uses the English verb *fuck* in Russian transliteration and with Russian morphological endings of a Russian reflexive verb – as if it were a Russian verb (such a verb does not exist). Still, it is understood, because the mechanism itself is not unusual in modern Russian – especially in colloquial and slang terms, as well as in professional jargons; such "Russian" words as *лейбл* (label), *кастинг* (casting), *шузы* (shoes), *дистрибьютор* (distributor), *провайдер* (provider), *чат* (chat), *реалити-шоу* (reality-show), *гламур* (glamour), and many others are used every day and are understood, many of them acquire Russian morphological endings (of a certain grammatical gender, number, and case): *гламур**ный*** (belonging to *glamour*; the English borrowing acquires the inflectional affixes of the Russian adjective); *трабл**ы*** (from the English word *troubles*) gets a plural ending of Russian nouns; *юз**ать*** (from the English verb *to use*) acquires a Russian infinitive ending, etc.

Neologisms

This is another rare case; still, I do have one anti-proverb that uses a verb that does not belong to standard Russian, nevertheless – since it follows the rules of word-formation – it is easily understood:

> TP: *Пролетарии всех стран, объединяйтесь!* (Workers of the world, unite!)
> AP: *Предприниматели всех стран, налогооблажайтесь!* (Entrepreneurs of the world, tax yourselves!)

The traditional saying is a well-known quotation from Karl Marx's "Communist Manifesto," while the new version is of course just a joke and encourages entrepreneurs to pay taxes. The key feature of the anti-proverb is the verb *налогооблажайтесь* (tax yourselves) that does not exist in Russian, though its meaning is clear, thanks to the fact that it uses a standard word-formation mechanism. Of course, it will hardly become a regular verb, but it serves its function well enough in this new version of Marx's slogan.

Lexical mechanisms:

- polysemy
- antonymy
- synonymy
- new lexical content of the same syntactic structure

Polysemy

Many anti-proverbs are coined by means of polysemy – two or more meanings of the same word, and quite a few of them were analyzed in the previous parts (for example, ##14, 51, 108, 155). Let us have a look at a couple of examples that were not discussed yet.

TP: *Сделал сам – помоги другому* (If you have finished your work, help another person).

AP: *Бросил курить сам, брось курить другому* (If you have quit smoking yourself, throw [a cigarette] to another person).

Once again, the literal translation means next to nothing: the AP uses the play on words based on two different meanings of the Russian verb *бросать* (literally, throw). In the phrase *бросить курить* it means *to quit smoking* (literally, throw smoking), but in the phrase *брось курить* (imperative of the same verb) it means *give* (literally, again, throw) *a cigarette* to another person. Since as a result the first and the second parts of this AP contradict each other, the resulting phrase is a very good example of the play on words based on polysemy.

Sometimes, the polysemantic word which is the basis of the play on words is used only once in a sentence, but both meanings are realized simultaneously, thus making the play (and the joke) even more evident:

AP: *Естественный отбор – это изъятие денег у мужа после получки* (Literally, Natural selection is taking away the husband's money on payday).

Once again, the literal translation makes no sense, because the Russian word *отбор*, though used only once, realizes two meanings together, which makes it a good joke: in the beginning of the sentence, which starts as a serious definition, the Russian phrase *естественный отбор* corresponds to the English term *natural selection*; but when one reads on it becomes clear that it is a wordplay based on the second meaning of the verbal noun *отбор* – taking away.

Another example where the polysemantic word is not repeated:

AP: *Чтобы выжить в России, одного терпения мало. Нужно два* (In order to survive in Russia, it is not enough to have only [one] patience: you need two).

The play on words here is based on the polysemantic phrase *одного терпения* (literally, *only patience*): the Russian word *одного* can also mean *one* in the genitive case; so when one reads this sentence of course the first meaning that is understood is, "It is not enough to have only patience" – that is, one needs something else. But the continuation utilizes the other meaning – "one patience," and makes it a sad joke: one needs two patience(s) to survive in Russia today.

Antonymy

Antonyms are words that have opposite meaning, and this device is used fairly often. Let me start with an example where *regular antonyms* are used (it was analyzed in # 95):

TP: *Настоящий мужчина должен посадить дерево, построить дом и вырастить сына* (A true man must plant a tree, build a house, and raise a son). This saying reflects the traditional (patriarchal) view of the duties of the man.

AP: *Настоящая женщина должна спилить дерево, разрушить дом и вырастить дочь* (A true woman must cut the tree, demolish the house and raise a daughter). One should not look for any deep meaning or wisdom in this AP; all it does is make fun of the patriarchal mores; the joke is obviously based on preserving the same structure (a true ___ must do three things), while listing antonyms: man – woman, plant a tree – cut a tree, build a house – demolish the house, son – daughter).

At the same time, it is quite common for anti-proverbs to use pairs of words as *contextual antonyms* – that is, antonyms that have opposite meaning only in the given context, but do not have opposite vocabulary meanings. Let us have a closer look at the AP that was analyzed in #125:

AP: *У плохого студента есть шанс стать хорошим солдатом* (A bad student has a chance to become a good soldier). This modern proverb reflects such a fact of soviet and Russian life as military draft: all male citizens who reach the age of 18 are eligible for the draft. Students of colleges and universities get an extension, and are drafted after they graduate. Thus, many people enter colleges and universities not because they want to get a higher education, but primarily to avoid being drafted into the army. As a result, quite a few students study poorly, as they are not interested in the specialty that they have chosen. Thus, if a student is expelled he is immediately drafted, hence the moral of the proverb: if you study poorly and get expelled you will be in the army. So the phrases (*плохой) студент* (bad student) and *(хороший) солдат* (good soldier) become contextual antonyms here, though, of course, by the dictionary definitions, they are not antonymous in any way.

Synonymy

Synonyms are words that have similar meanings and can replace each other at least in some contexts. They may differ in the components of their conceptual meaning, or in their stylistic and emotional connotations. In my examples, there are cases of stylistic synonymy (#10), as well as cases of contextual synonyms (## 6, 9).

Stylistic synonyms
TP: *По одежке встречают, по уму провожают* (One is greeted by the clothes, and seen off by the mind). Figuratively, it

is similar to the English saying *Appearances are deceptive*; *Beauty is only skin deep*, etc., thus, we first judge people by the way they look, and later on, when we learn more about them, we judge them by their inner world.

AP: *По прикиду встречают, по понятиям провожают* (One is greeted by the clothes, and seen off by the street laws). The meaning is very much the same, but stylistically the wording is completely different. The association with the original proverb is achieved by preserving the structure and both verbs of the original proverb (*По _____ встречают, по _____ провожают*), though stylistically the AP belongs to the low colloquial register, having replaced the key nouns by their stylistic synonyms: *по одежке* (TP) – *по прикиду* (AP), and *по уму* (TP) – *по понятиям* (AP).

Contextual synonyms

TP: *Дружба дружбой, а табачок врозь* (Though we are friends, I am not going to share my tobacco with you). Figuratively, it means that there are limits to what friends will do for each other.

AP: *Дружба дружбой, а нефть врозь* (Though we are friends, I am not going to share my oil with you). Figurative meaning is absent.

The AP is another reflection of modern Russian realities, where oil companies compete for oil deposits and federal government support. The association with the traditional proverb is achieved by the same syntactic pattern and common wording, except one word: *oil* (in AP) as opposed to *tobacco* in the TP. The use of the word *табак* (tobacco) in TP is not accidental: it reflects the traditional high value of tobacco in Russia, hence, unwillingness to share it even with friends. And since oil in modern Russia is as valuable a possession as tobacco was in old days, this is a good example of contextual synonymy.

TP: *Ниже пояса не бить* (Do not hit below the belt). This is one of the rules of the honest fight; figuratively, it can also mean any kind of "fight" which is done according to established rules, not necessarily physical fighting.

AP: *Ниже пейджера не бить* (Do not hit below the pager); the meaning is the same, as a pager is kept on the belt. This is an interesting example of new wording for a traditional wisdom; the words *пояс* (belt) *пейджер* (pager) are used as contextual synonyms, as they both indicate the same area of the human body.

New lexical content of the same syntactic structure (partial or complete)

This device is used very often, and it is not by chance that in the previous analysis there were numerous examples of modern anti-proverbs that copy the syntactical structure of their prototype, but fill it with new words, either replacing all the words or some of them (sometimes changing just one word; see for example, ## 10, 36, 47). Let us have a look at some new examples, ranging from one new word and up to a completely new (lexically) sentence.

TP: *Молчание – знак согласия* (Silence means agreement).
AP: *Венчание – знак согласия* (Wedding means agreement).

The traditional proverb expresses an old wisdom: when a person you are talking to is silent when you have suggested something, it means that that person agrees with you.

In the new version, the word *молчание* (silence) is replaced with the word *венчание* (wedding) and of course means a completely different thing: if you have a wedding, it means that the other person agrees to marry you.

Let me give one more interesting example of a new lexical filling of a well-known syntactical structure.

TP: *Я милого узнаю по походке* (I will recognize my dear by the way he walks [this is a girl talking, because the adjective *милого* (dear) is used in the masculine form]).
AP: *Я милую узнаю по колготкам* (I will recognize my dear by the pantyhose [obviously, a man is speaking; besides, the word *милую* (dear) is used in the feminine form here]).

One should not look for some deep sense here. The original sentence is the first line of a very popular song (the author of the lyrics is unknown), known to the majority of people. The AP is one more language joke: by replacing *милого* (dear in the masculine) by *милую* (dear in the feminine), and by changing *по походке* (by the way he walks) to *по колготкам* (by pantyhose; these two rhyme in the Russian sentences) it will simply cause people to laugh or at least smile.

Sometimes, it is enough to replace just a form word (like a preposition) not only to change the meaning of a proverb, but to create a completely different moral (#24):

TP: *Мойте руки перед едой* (Wash your hands before eating). This is a well-known slogan propagating public hygiene, and known by everyone since one's childhood.
AP: *Мойте руки вместо еды* (Wash your hands instead of eating).
The meaning of this AP is a reflection of modern-day realities: a large part of the population cannot afford to buy enough food; thus, if you have no food, all you can do is to perform the first part of the procedure: wash your hands. The language device used here is the change of prepos-ition: *перед* (before) is replaced by *вместо* (instead of).

The same trick is the basis of another sad joke (#23):

TP: *Аппетит приходит во время еды* (Appetite comes with eating).
AP: *Аппетит приходит вместо еды* (Appetite comes instead of eating).
This is another reflection of the sad reality: there can be nothing to eat, either because people have no money to buy food, or because, especially in transition time, there was scarcity of goods in grocery stores. Now, of course, it is mostly the first: food prices sky-rocketed in recent years (2007-2008), and the low income population[36] literally cannot afford to buy basic food items.

The extreme version of this mechanism is the case when nearly all the lexical content of a familiar saying is replaced, for example (#26):

TP: *В человеке все должно быть прекрасно: и лицо, и одежда, и душа, и мысли.* (Everything must be beautiful in a man: the face, the clothes. the soul, and the thoughts).
This is a well-known quotation from the play *Uncle Vanya* by Anton Chekhov.
AP: *В бизнесмене все должно быть прекрасно: и 600-й мерс, и дача на Канарах, и контрольный выстрел в голову* (Everything must be beautiful in a businessman: his Mercedes, his vacation home in Canary Islands, and his control bullet in the head).

Thus, the new version has a completely new wording, except the introductory phrase: *все должно быть прекрасно* (everything must be beautiful). Thus, it is new content per se that creates a new proverb reflecting modern-day realities: no one can feel safe, no matter how rich he or she is.

Here is another example where only one word is left from the original proverb (#48):

TP: *Не место красит человека, а человек место* (It is not the place that adorns the man, but the man who adorns the place.) The obvious meaning is that what you are is much more important than the things that surround you or that you possess.
AP: *Не одежда красит девушку, а отсутствие оной!* (It is not the clothes that adorn the girl, but their absence). Once again, the original meaning is lost, so in this respect this AP is nothing new. But what is new is its form. This time, the deviation from the TP is quite substantial: in fact, only one word – *красит* (adorns) is left intact.

Somewhere in between are examples when the new version replaces some key words of the original proverb but keeps the rest (#38):

TP: *Редкая птица долетит до середины Днепра* (It is a rare bird that can fly till the middle of the Dnepr river). This is a well-known description of the Dnepr River from the novel *Dead Souls* by Nikolay Gogol.

AP: *Редкий премьер долетит до середины Атлантики* (It is a rare prime-minister that can fly till the middle of the Atlantic Ocean).

The original quotation is easily recognized thanks to the same syntactic structure and partly the same wording: *Редкая/ая _____ долетит до середины _____* (It is a rare _____ that can fly till the middle of _____).

Syntactic mechanisms:

- restructuring
- extension

Syntactic restructuring

This device is used quite rarely as compared to many others, but nevertheless it presents an interesting case: by restructuring the original syntax, an anti-proverb creates a new meaning while leaving the lexical content intact. For example (I analyzed this case in more detail in #69):

TP: *Мусор из избы не выносить* (Do not carry your garbage out of the house). This is an interesting example of old advice which became a proverb: traditional prejudices required not to take the garbage outside, but burn it in the stove, as it was believed that an evil person could bring bad luck to the house saying some special words about the garbage.

AP: *Мусора, из избы не выносить* (Cops, do not carry [me] out of the house). This joke is based on the coincidence of the two Russian words: *мусор* (garbage) in the original proverb, and *мусор* (slang for policeman) in the anti-proverb. But more importantly, the syntactic structure is also changed in the AP, and even both sentences are imperative constructions, in the AP *мусора* is the address, not the object of the action *carry out*. Thus, we are dealing with a situation when police officers come to somebody's home and the drunken person says to them: cops, do not carry me out of the house; leave me alone. Thus, by restructuring the original phrase an old proverb becomes a language joke by means of the different syntax:

TP: Object – adverbial of place – verb
AP: Address – adverbial of place – verb

Let us have a look at another example (#74):

116

TP: *Унылая пора,* (очей очарованье!) (Melancholy time, so charming to the eye!) This is a well-known quotation from Alexander Pushkin's poem "Autumn."

AP: *Унылая, пора* (Melancholy, [it is] time [to go]). The original saying is restructured: first, the modifier *унылая* (melancholy) has become the address in the AP: the speaker asks his girl-friend (this is marked by the feminine ending of the adjective): [my] melancholy [girl], it is time to go! Also, the second word, *пора,* though it looks the same on the surface, is different, as well: in the TP it is a noun and means "time of the year"; in the AP it is an adverb with the "it is time to go." Thus, the relationships of the TP and AP are very complex, even though both consist of two words only: the form (succession of phonemes) is the same, but the syntactic structure is different:

TP: Adjective (modifier) + noun
AP: Address + adverbial modifier of time

Extension of syntactic structure

Even though there is a special pattern which uses extension of the original structure as the mechanism of creating anti-proverbs, there is still a need to analyze syntactic extension separately, as it is often an umbrella device covering quite a few different things. In other words, it is quite rare that extension of the syntactic structure is used as the only mechanism of creating a new proverb; much more often, it is just a vehicle for other more obvious means – lexical, phonetic, stylistic, etc. So let us have a look at a couple of examples where *syntax* itself is the key method used to create an anti-proverb.

Here is an example that was discussed earlier (#107):

TP: *Курить вредно* (Smoking is bad for your health). This is a popular common sense maxim.

AP: *Курить вредно, пить противно, а умирать здоровым – жалко* (Smoking is bad, drinking is disgusting, but dying healthy is a pity.) This AP, after listing serious undisputable facts, makes an unexpected conclusion: since everyone dies no matter whether one drinks and smokes or not, why not drink and smoke?

One more example (#100):

TP: *В вине мудрость* (In wine there is wisdom). This is a Russian translation of the old Latin maxim, *In vino veritas*.

AP: *В вине мудрость, в пиве – сила, в воде – микробы* (In wine there is wisdom, in beer – power, in water – microbes). This joking extension, using the true fact (there are quite a few dangerous microbes in unfiltered water), twists it in such a way that it turns out that the most useful drinks are wine and beer, as they do not have any microbes!

Stylistic mechanisms:

- metaphor
- metonymy
- oxymoron
- chiasmus
- anadiplosis
- wellerism

These figures of speech are used to create modern Russian anti-proverbs. Let us have a look at some examples.

Metaphor

Metaphor is the understanding of one concept in terms of another, based on their similarity. I cannot say that it is often used, but I do have a couple of very good examples (#139 and 99):

AP: *Свадьба – это контрольный выстрел Амура* (Wedding is the control shot of Amor). *Control shot* is the jargon of professional killers; this is a shot in the head to make sure that the victim is dead, not just wounded. Here, it is used metaphorically: wedding plays the same role in relationships between a man and a woman: it makes sure that the man is caught for life.

TP: *Дети – цветы жизни* (Children are flowers of life). This is a well-known quotation from Maxim Gorky (from his story "Former People," written in 1897). Often used as emphasizing the importance of children in life of any person, and of the society in general. As I have already mentioned, this TP gave birth to 16 anti-proverbs; all of them are based on the play of words: *flowers* used in their literal meaning, and *flowers* meaning *children*, according to Gorky's metaphoric phrase. For example:
AP: *Дети – цветы жизни. Дарите девушкам цветы.* (Children are flowers of life. Give flowers to girls.) This is just a joke, based on the play of literal and figurative meanings.

Metonymy

Metonymy is another name for an object based on some connections between them (special, causal, part and whole, etc.). Let us have a look at two examples (##3, 5):

TP: *Долг платежом красен* (The debt is made red by the payment). The literal meaning is that one should promptly return the money one owes to somebody. Figuratively, it can also mean that anything that you owe someone (not necessarily money) should be promptly returned.

AP: *Долг платежом зелен* (The debt is made green by the payment). The literal meaning is the same; figurative meaning is absent.

In the TP, the adjective *red*, is used in its old meaning – "beautiful, good looking" (thus, for instance, Red Square in Moscow is, of course, "beautiful square," not square red in color). Thus, *the debt is made red by the payment* means that it is good (morally correct) to pay your debts, both monetary and others.

Green is quite opposite in its etymology, and originates in the realities of modern Russian economy, where the dollar, especially in the early 90s, was considered the most reliable currency. Since dollar bills are green, the AP uses metonymy and in fact says that one should pay one's debts in dollars.

TP: *Гусь свинье не товарищ* (A goose and a pig cannot be friends). Figuratively, persons from different spheres of life cannot have anything in common.

AP: *Евро баксу не товарищ* (Euro and dollar cannot be friends). Figurative meaning is absent.

Once again, the anti-proverb, using the syntactical pattern of the traditional proverb, expresses the same (literal) meaning by means of the new realities, because really, in the sphere of economic relationships, the euro (that is, European economy) and the dollar (that is, US economy) are competitors, not friends. The association of the AP and the TP is achieved by the same syntactic frame and partly the same wording: .... *cannot be friends.*

This is a classic example of metonymy (*pars pro toto*: part – dollar, euro – representing whole (economy).

Oxymoron

Oxymoron is figure of speech based on a logical contradiction; here is an example that was discussed in #141:

AP: *Самый лучший способ запомнить день рождения жены – один раз его забыть* (The best way to remember your wife's birthday is to forget it once). Again, on the surface we have a logical contradiction: how can one remember by forgetting? At the same time, there is no contradiction here, because if one forgets about his wife's birthday once, there will be such a scandal that the poor husband will remember that day forever.

This anti-proverb was also analyzed earlier (#143):

AP: *Как врачи его ни лечили, он все равно выздоровел* (No matter how the doctors tried to treat him, the patient recovered). First we are told that the doctors did their best to cure the patient, but in vain; so we expect a bad end, but we are wrong, as the patient managed to survive in spite of the treatment; thus, it is an oxymoron that is the basis for the humor.

Chiasmus

Chiasmus is an inverted relationship between the syntactic elements of parallel phrases. Let us have a look at a couple of examples (#117 and 109):

TP: *Собака – друг человека* (A dog is a man's friend). This is a popular (and true) description of dogs.
AP: *Хорошо, когда собака – друг, но плохо, когда друг – собака* (It is good when your dog is a friend, but it is bad when your friend is a dog). The humor is lost in translation: the Russian word "dog," when applied to people, has a negative connotation. Thus, it means that when your friend turns out to be a bad person, this is bad. The saying is well coined, as on the surface,

thanks to the double meaning of the word *dog*, it is symmetrical, and the second part is a mirror image of the first. Thus, the AP is a good example of chiasmus used to create a new wisdom.

TP: *Молитва – это разговор с Богом* (Prayer is a talk with God). This is a commonly accepted understanding of what a prayer is.

AP: *Когда ты говоришь с Богом – это молитва. Когда Бог с тобой – это шизофрения.* (When you talk to God, this is a prayer. When God talks to you, this is schizophrenia.) The extension, by changing the subject and the object in the subordinate clause, makes this unexpected (though from the point of view of a psychiatrist, probably logical) conclusion. Obviously, it has nothing to do with the original saying, but the mechanisms of making this joke is another case of chiasmus.

Anadiplosis

Anadiplosis is repetition of the last prominent word of a clause in the next one, with an adjunct idea. I have only one, but a very good example of this stylistic device (#87):

TP: *Дуракам закон не писан* (Fools recognize no laws). This traditional expression is used in situations when someone does a clearly foolish thing, often even detrimental to one, and thus, someone will say, *Fools recognize no laws*, meaning, what can you do with such a person?

AP: *Дуракам закон не писан. А если писан, то не читан. А если читан, то не понят. А если понят, то не так.* (Fools recognize no laws. And if they recognize them, they have not read them. And even if they have read them, they have not understood them. And if they have understood them, they understood them in the wrong way.) This is a very interesting example of stylistic development of a traditional proverb: anadiplosis does not change the meaning much and only emphasizes that no mater what fools do, they will never understand any commonly accepted rules of human society.

Wellerism

This type of stylistic device, based on the wordplay involving a metaphorical and literal sense, got its name after Sam Weller – Mr. Pickwick's witty servant in Charles Dickens's novel *The Posthumous Papers of the Pickwick Club*. Sam was fond of following well-known sayings by his own conclusions. Soon after publication of the novel (1836-1837), such witticisms started to be called *wellerisms*.

There are two examples of wellerisms in my corpus, and both were discussed earlier (#90 and #114):

TP: *Какой же русский не любит быстрой езды!* (What Russian is not fond of driving fast!) This quotation is taken from the novel *Dead Souls* by the famous Russian writer Nikolay Gogol (1809-1852).

AP: *"Какой же новый русский не любит быстрой езды?" сказал гаишник, пересчитывая бабки* ("What new Russian is not fond of driving fast?" said the policeman counting the money.)

The new version, as was already mentioned, is one more allusion to modern Russian mores (see my analysis of #90). At the same time, this AP clearly follows the structure of wellerisms, as it uses the play on words comparing a well-known quotation to a facetious sequel.

TP: *От сумы да от тюрьмы не зарекайся* (No one can be sure that he will not be poor or get in jail). This old proverb teaches that human life is unpredictable, and no matter what one's current position in life is, one cannot be sure what will happen tomorrow.

AP: *От сумы да от тюрьмы не зарекайся, - говорит кенгуру в зоопарке* (No one can be sure that he will not be poor or get in jail, said the kangaroo in the zoo). This extension is based on the play on words: the literal Russian wording of the original proverb is: No one can say that he will not have a [beggar's] bag or get in jail.

Since the kangaroo is in a zoo, and has a kind of bag (the pocket on its belly), it has both the bag and is behind bars; thus, it punningly confirms the old maxim in the form of a wellerism.

Defeated expectancy

Defeated expectancy stands aside from the rest of this chapter. The thing is that it is not a mechanism of creating some (stylistic, ironic, emphatic) effect, but rather the result of some other device. The reason I thought it necessary to analyze it separately is the fact that defeated expectancy is a key feature of many anti-proverbs (in fact, the reason for creating many of them), so it makes sense to see how this effect is achieved.

The device itself is a very old one and is traditionally used to attract attention of the reader to some element of the text that receives prominence due to an interruption in the pattern of predictability. In other words, it is based on the fact that usually the reader, on the basis of his or her background, general knowledge, or previous context expects to see a continuation that makes sense (predictable); so when this expectation is ruined, the result is an additional emphasis on the part that is surprising. Of course, it is mostly used to create language jokes instead of some serious or traditional maxim, but is also used as a stylistic device in poetry. Just to give a classic example, it is the essence of the well-known poem "November" written by British poet Thomas Hood (1799-1845):

No sun – no moon!
No morn – no noon!
No dawn – no dusk – no proper time of day –
No sky – no earthly view –
No distance looking blue –
....
No warmth, no cheerfulness, no healthful ease,
No comfortable feel in any member –
No shade, no shine, no butterflies, no bees,
No fruits, no flowers, no leaves, no birds! –
November!

The last line – November! – receives prominence exactly because by the time the reader reaches it, he or she expects one more negation, and the first syllable of the word *November* seems to confirm this expectation – only to show that the reader's expectancy will be immediately defeated.

In the current analysis, there have been many examples of this stylistic device; see, for example, ## 72, 83, 134. Before examining several new ones, let me remind the reader a couple of the anti-proverbs that were discussed earlier (##78, 88,145):

TP: *Всех денег не заработаешь* (One cannot earn all the money). This is an old expression, usually said to someone who is dedicating all the time to earning more and more money. It is a common sense maxim, which says: no matter how much you can earn, there will be much more money that one has not earned, while one is spending (or as many will say, wasting) life on that, depriving oneself of many other aspects of life. Thus, the moral of this saying is not that it is bad to earn money, but rather that one should not dedicate all life to that.

AP: *Всех денег не заработаешь – часть придется украсть* (One cannot earn all the money – some money will have to be stolen). As we can see, the extension gives the proverb a new meaning, and is quite alien to the original one. The way to do this is standard for this pattern – the extension creates a completely new context, so the old, traditional, part acquires a new meaning, as well: now the beginning (*One cannot earn all the money*) is not a warning that there are other aspects of life which one can miss if dedicating all the time to money, but rather a justification of stealing; since it is impossible to earn money anyway, there is no other choice but to steal some part of it. Thus, this AP is a great example of defeated expectancy, built on the fact that the familiar maxim gets a completely new interpretation due to the extension (some money will have to be stolen).

TP: *Лежачего не бьют* (One should not hit a person lying on the ground). This is a traditional rule of fair fight: two people will hit each other until one falls down, but it is unfair to keep hitting someone who is lying on the ground.

AP: *Никогда не бей лежачего: ведь он может встать* (Never hit a person lying on the ground: he may stand up). Again, the extension gives the original saying a completely new meaning: instead of being one of the rules of the fair fight, it becomes a warning to be careful, as the person who is lying may stand up and hit you back. Thus, this AP is another great example of defeated expectancy.

AP: *О вреде курения пишут так много, что я твердо решил бросить читать* (There are so many books about the harm of smoking that I decided to give up reading). Up to the very end, the reader is sure that this is one more confession of a person who is convinced that smoking is damaging for health, and decided to give up. But the last word shows that this is not the case: the person decided to give up reading, not smoking, as reading all these horror stories upsets him. As a result, defeated expectancy at its best.

Now let us have a look at some new ones.

TP: *Курица не птица, Болгария не заграница* (Chicken is not a bird, Bulgaria is not abroad).

AP: *Курица не птица, курица это еда такая* (Chicken is not a bird, chicken is a type of food).

The traditional saying reflects one of the realities of the soviet times: on the one hand, the relationships between the USSR and Bulgaria were so close that it was often considered the 16th soviet republic.[37] It was believed that had it not been for Rumania that separated the USSR and Bulgaria it would have joined the Soviet Union. On the other hand, since it was next to impossible for the soviet citizens to travel abroad, Bulgaria was one of the very few opportunities to actually go to some other country (usually, for vacations on the Bulgarian coast of the Black Sea). Hence, this saying that reflected those realities: one could visit Bulgaria and thus technically could go abroad, but in fact one still remained within the soviet block.

The new version breaks this familiar expression making it formally a definition and in reality simply a joke: chicken is not a bird, it is a type of food. To a person who has lived in the Soviet Union, this creates defeated expectancy, as one expects the familiar ending of this popular saying, but I am afraid the younger generation will miss the point completely.

TP: *Деньги – зло* (Money is evil).

AP: *Деньги – зло. Причините мне его побольше.* (Money is evil. Bring me as much as possible of it.)

Once again, the traditional phrase is a commonly used expression characterizing money as the source of evil. The AP, which starts in the same way, at first produces the impression that the continuation will provide further development of the same idea, but the reality is exactly the opposite: the narrator asks to give him as much of this evil (that is, money) as possible.

And finally – a very new anti-proverb (published on the Web in May 2008), marking the end of Vladimir Putin's presidency:

AP: *Запад пытался поставить Россию на колени, но она продолжала лежать...* (The West was trying to make Russia stand on her knees, but she continued to lie…).

Once again, to understand the black humor of this recent coinage, one needs to know some background information. During the presidency of Vladimir Putin, one of the key propaganda ideas was the idea that western countries are trying to subjugate Russia and make her an inferior country, so Russia needs to take some measures to counter this tendency.

The well-known phrase "make somebody stand on the knees" means to make a person (or another country) subordinate to another (person or country). Thus, the AP starts as a standard anti-west propaganda (the West was trying to make Russia stand on her knees), so the reader expects, in the same way, a traditional ending (for instance, *but our leadership did not allow that to happen*, or, *but the new Russia is an independent and powerful country*, and so on). Instead, the new wisdom creates an unexpected punch line – but she continued to lie on the ground – which, of course, besides being a sad joke, also contains a sharp criticism of the current Russian government and its foreign policy.

Combination of different mechanisms

Even though it may sound obvious, my last item is the situation when anti-proverbs use a combination of several devices. Let us have a look at several examples.

Internal rhyme and hidden rhyme (#25):

TP: *Не зная броду, не суйся в воду* (If you do not know the place of the ford, do not go into the water; similar to the English, *Look before your leap*).

AP: *Не зная броду, не ври народу* (If you do not know the place of the ford, do not lie to your people).

As one can see, the AP has internal rhyme (as the TP does) and it also has hidden rhyme, as *народу* (in the AP) and *в воду* (in the TP) rhyme. So, to truly appreciate the new coinage, one has to recognize the original proverb in it, which the hidden rhyme helps to do.

Syntactic restructuring and homonymy (#69):

TP: *Мусор из избы не выносить* (Do not carry your garbage out of the house).

AP: *Мусора, из избы не выносить* (Cops, do not carry [me] out of the house).

Homonymy: *мусор* in the TP means *garbage*; the same word in AP means (in slang) *a cop*.

Syntactic restructuring:

TP: Object – adverbial of place – verb
AP: Address – adverbial of place – verb

Paronymy and hidden rhyme (#44):

TP: *Что посеешь, то и пожнешь* (As you sow you shall mow; similar to the English Bible proverb, *As you sow you shall reap*). Obviously, this proverb speaks not only about sowing and mowing; its figurative meaning is much broader: the consequences of one's actions depend entirely on the actions themselves.

AP: *Что посмеешь, то и пожмешь* (As you dare you shall grasp). Once again, the change of one phoneme changes the meaning completely: the figurative meaning disappears, while the literal meaning has nothing to do with the original proverb, and sounds more like a joking piece of advice. Linguistically, this is achieved by replacing the two verbs in the TP by two paronyms, but that is not all: the new verbs rhyme with the verbs in the original proverb.

Polysemy and paronymy (#77):

TP: *Уходя, гасите свет* (When leaving, switch off the lights). Any Russian person has seen this slogan many times and in many places.

AP: *Уходя, гасите всех* (When leaving, eliminate everyone).

Even though short, the new version uses quite complicated language means: first, it has the verb *гасить* (literally, switch off) used in the slang meaning, *to kill*. Thus, even though the first two words, from the point of view of their form, are the same both in the TP and AP, the second word (the verb) is in fact used in a different meaning, and this difference in meaning is, as usual, indicated by the context. In the original expression, the object is an inanimate thing, *light*; hence it is clear that the verb is used in its direct meaning. In the second, the object *everyone* is, of course, animate, hence, it is clear that the verb cannot be used in the literal meaning. Secondly, the AP uses paronymic relations between the Russian words *свет* (light) and *всех* (everyone). Even though they do differ, they both are one-syllable words, and both are stressed and have three phonemes in common (though their order is different): [s], [v], and [e].

Polysemy and hidden rhyme (#62):

TP: *Он сказал: «Поехали!» И взмахнул рукой.* (He said: Let's go! And waved his hand.) "Let's go!" is the famous exclamation used by the first cosmonaut Yuri Gagarin when he was launched into space on April 12, 1961.

AP: *Он сказал: «Поехали!» И запил водой.* (He said: Let's go! And washed down with water.)

The first part of the TP and the first part of the AP only look the same; the reason is that the phrase "let's go" has two meanings: (1) it can have its literal meaning, that is, one will say this phrase when one starts on a journey, or a trip, (2) it is used as a short toast while drinking; thus, "Let's go" means "Let's drink." As is usual with polysemantic words and expressions, the meaning becomes evident in the context. Besides, *запил водой* (washed down with water) rhymes with *взмахнул рукой* (waved his hand) in the original phrase. Thus, the AP uses both polysemy and hidden rhyme.

Finally, an example of an anti-proverb that has three mechanisms: *paronymy, metonymy,* and *hidden rhyme* (#13):

TP: *Поживем – увидим* (We shall live and see) – usually said to people who are very sure in their predictions of the results of their actions.

AP: *Пожуем – увидим* (We shall chew and see). The figurative meaning is the same, as chewing (that is, eating – a great example of metonymy) is, in its turn, part of living; so again, double metonymy, allowing the AP to preserve the original meaning in spite of the change of one of the two verbs.

Besides, the AP is nearly 100% homophonic with the traditional proverb: the Russian verbs *поживем* ([we] *shall live*) and *пожуем* ([we] *shall chew*) are paronyms, as they coincide in their phonetic structure except one phoneme; and because of that, they rhyme, so the AP has a hidden rhyme, as well.

This list can be continued, but the main idea is that it is quite common for modern Russian anti-proverbs to use more than one device to create either a new moral or simply a new wordplay – or both.

5. Conclusion: Anti-Proverbs or Modern Proverbs?

Modern Russian anti-proverbs are a diverse group. They are different in many aspects: their origin, their relationships with the traditional proverbs, their usage, the language mechanisms used in their creation, and their chances of survival and staying in the language.

The analysis of the proverbs of the soviet period shows that the phenomenon of anti-proverbs is not something either unique or new for the Russian language. Every epoch produces its own anti-proverbs, and this is especially true for a historic period when abrupt changes take place in the society.

Many anti-proverbs confirm old truths and express old wisdom in a new way or by new means. They show that proverbs are not something complete and never changing, but in fact are as changeable a part of the language as anything else.

Other anti-proverbs use familiar patterns to express new truths, thus reflecting not only new events or aspects of the modern society and people but also new mores. Those of them that (in terms of their form) follow the best traditions of Russian proverbs have all the chances of staying in the language. As traditional proverbs show, even when the realities that produced them disappear, the proverbs survive due to their figurative meaning and their expressing folk wisdom that has diachronic character.

At the same time, many modern anti-proverbs are just language jokes or wordplays created for fun, and will hardly survive, especially if their form is awkward.

So, are anti-proverbs simply modern proverbs, that is, are they old wine in new bottles? As I hope my research showed, there is no simple answer to this question

Some of the anti-proverbs confirm old truths using new forms, so they are, indeed, *old* wine in *new* bottles.

Some other modern anti-proverbs express new wisdom using traditional forms, thus, they are, in fact, just the opposite phenomenon: they are *new* wine in *old* bottles.

Still other anti-proverbs express new wisdom or reflect new realities using new forms, so they are *new* wine in *new* bottles.

Which of these bottles will stay and preserve the wine that is inside remains to be seen, but as I hope the analysis has shown, there are good chances for some of the old wine to stay in new bottles, and the new wine in old bottles, as well as some of the new wine in new bottles.

Appendix

Index of the anti-proverbs analyzed in the book

Pattern I: Similar Form – Same Wisdom

	Traditional Proverb	Anti-Proverb	Language Mechanism
1.	*Куй железо, пока горячо.* Strike the iron while it is hot.	*Куй железо, пока Горбачев.* Strike the iron while Gorbachev.	Paronymy, hidden rhyme
2.	*Волков бояться в – лес не ходить.* If you are afraid of wolves do not go to the forest.	*Путина бояться – в сортир не ходить.* If you are afraid of Putin do not go to the outhouse.	Contextual synonymy
3.	*Долг платежом красен.* The debt is made red by the payment.	*Долг платежом зелен.* The debt is made green by the payment.	Metonymy, polysemy
4.	*Храните деньги в сберегательных кассах!* Keep your money in the savings banks!	*Храните деньги в сберегательных баксах!* Keep your money in the savings bucks!	Hidden rhyme
5.	*Гусь свинье не товарищ.* A goose and a pig cannot be friends.	*Евро баксу не товарищ.* Euro and dollar cannot be friends.	Metonymy

6.	*Дружба дружбой, а табачок врозь.* Though we are friends, I am not going to share my to-bacco with you.	*Дружба дружбой, а нефть врозь.* Though we are friends, I am not going to share my oil with you.	Contextual synonymy
7.	*Семь бед – один ответ.* Seven problems – one answer.	*Семь бед – один reset* Seven problems – one reset.	Hidden rhyme
8.	*Скажи мне, кто твой друг, и я скажу тебе, кто ты.* Tell me who your friend is, and I will tell you who you are.	*Скажи мне, что ты ешь, и я скажу тебе, кто ты.* Tell me what you eat, and I will tell you who you are.	New lexical content of the same syntactic structure
9.	*Ниже пояса не бить.* Do not hit below the belt.	*Ниже пейджера не бить.* Do not hit below the pager.	Contextual synonyms
10.	*По одежке встречают, по уму провожают.* One is greeted by the clothes, and seen off by	*По прикиду встречают, по понятиям провожают.* One is greeted by the clothes, and seen off by the	Stylistic synonyms

	the mind.	street laws.	
11.	*Не говори гоп, пока не пере- прыгнешь.* Do not say "gop" until you jump over. (English equivalent: *There is many a slip between the cup and the lip.*)	*Не говори гоп, пока не пере- едешь Чоп.* Do not say "gop" until you pass Chop.	Internal rhyme
12.	*Двое пашут, а семеро руками машут.* Two people are plowing, and seven people are waving hands.	*Кто пашет, а кто с Мавзолея рукой машет.* Some are plow- ing, and some others are waving their hands from the Mausoleum.	Internal rhyme
13.	*Поживем – увидим* We shall live and see.	*Пожуем – уви- дим* We shall chew and see.	Paronymy, me- tonymy, hidden rhyme
14.	*Не переходи- те улицу на красный свет.* Do not cross the street when the light is red.	*Не переходите улицу на тот свет.* Do not cross the street to the other world.	Homonymy
15a.	*Чем бы дитя ни тешилось, лишь бы не*	*Чем бы дитя ни тешилось, лишь бы не какало.*	Hidden rhyme

	плакало. Whatever the child plays with, the most important thing is that it does not cry.	Whatever the child plays with, most important is that it does not poop.	
15b.		*Чем бы дитя ни тешилось, лишь бы не факалось.* Whatever the child plays with, most important is that it does not fuck.	Internal rhyme, English verb in the Russian transliteration and with Russian inflexion.
16.	*Назвался груздем, полезай в кузов.* If you said you are a mushroom, get into the basket.	*Назвался клизмой, полезай в попу.* If you said you are a clyster, get into the anus.	Contextual synonyms
17.	*Снявши голову, по волосам не плачут.* When you lost your head, you do not cry over your hair.	*Снявши штаны, по волосам не гладят.* When you took off your pants, you do not stroke [your girlfriend's] hair.	Polysemy
18.	*Счастливые часов не наблюдают.* The happy do not notice the	*Счастливые трусов не одевают.* The happy do not put on under-	Double hidden rhyme

	time.	wear.	
19.	*Птицу видно по полету.* The bird is seen by its flight.	*Птицу видно по помету.* The bird is seen by its droppings.	Hidden rhyme

Pattern II: Similar Form – New Wisdom

	Traditional Proverb	Anti-Proverb	Language Mechanism
20a.	Долг платежом красен. The debt is made red by the payment.	Долг утюгом страшен. The debt is made scary by the iron.	Hidden rhyme
20b.		Долг процентом красен. The debt is made red by the interest.	Change of one word
21.	Тише едешь – дальше будешь. The slower you go, the farther you will get.	Водитель, помни: тише едешь – никому не должен. Driver, remember: the slower you go, the less you owe to anyone.	New lexical content of the same syntactic structure; extension of the original proverb
22.	Плачет девочка в автомате. A girl is crying in the phone booth.	Плачет девочка в банкомате. A girl is crying near the ATM.	Hidden rhyme
23a.	Аппетит приходит во время еды. Appetite comes with eating; the original proverb is a calque from French L'appetit	Аппетит приходит вместо еды. Appetite comes instead of eating.	Change of one word (preposition)

	vient en mangeant. This proverb is also found in English, *Appetite comes while eating.*	
23b.		*Гепатит приходит во время еды* Hepatitis comes with eating.	Hidden rhyme
24.	*Мойте руки перед едой.* Wash your hands before eating.	*Мойте руки вместо еды.* Wash your hands instead of eating.	Change of one word (preposition)
25.	*Не зная броду, не суйся в воду.* If you do not know the place of the ford, do not go into the water; similar to the English, *Look before your leap.*	*Не зная броду, не ври народу.* If you do not know the place of the ford, do not lie to your people.	Hidden rhyme; internal rhyme
26.	*В человеке все должно быть прекрасно: и лицо, и одежда, и душа, и мысли.* Everything must be beautiful in a man: the face, the clothes, the soul, and the thoughts.	*В бизнесмене все должно быть прекрасно: и 600-й мерс, и дача на Канарах, и контрольный выстрел в голову.* Everything must be beautiful in a businessman: his	New lexical content of the same syntactic structure.

140

		Mercedes, his vacation home in Canary Islands, and his control bullet in the head.	
27.	*Почем опиум для народа?* How much is opium for the people?	*Почем пентиум для народа?* How much is Pentium for the people?	Hidden rhyme
28a.	*Не имей сто рублей, а имей сто друзей.* Do not have a hundred rubles, but have a hundred friends.	*Не имей сто рублей, а женись как Аджубей.* Do not have a hundred rubles, but marry as Adjubey did.	Hidden rhyme; internal rhyme
28b.		*Не имей сто рублей, а имей сто баксов.* Do not have a hundred rubles, but have a hundred bucks.	Change of one word
29.	*Счастье – это когда тебя понимают.* Happiness – it is when you are understood.	*Переоценка ценностей: счастье – это когда тебя нанимают.* Change of values: happiness – it is when you are hired.	Hidden rhyme

30.	*Хочешь жить – умей вертеться.* If you want to live, you should be able to spin.	*Хочешь жить – умей раздеться.* If you want to live, you should be able to undress.	Hidden rhyme
31.	*И скучно, и грустно, и некому руку подать.* I am bored, and sad, and have no one to shake hands with.	*И скучно, и грустно, и некому тело продать.* I am bored, and sad, and have no one to sell my body to.	Hidden rhyme
32.	*Точность – вежливость королей.* Accuracy is the politeness of the kings.	*Точность – вежливость снайперов.* Accuracy is the politeness of the snipers.	Change of one word
33.	*Язык до Киева доведет.* Talking will get you to Kiev.	*Язык до киллера доведет.* Talking will get you to a killer [i.e., get killed].	Paronymy
34.	*Будешь много знать – скоро состаришься.* If you know too much you will get old quickly.	*Будешь много знать – не успеешь состариться.* If you know too much you will not be able to get old.	New lexical content of the same syntactic structure (change of one word)
35.	*Богата талантами земля на-*	*Богата зарытыми таланта-*	Adding one word

	ша! Rich in talents is our land!	ми земля наша! Rich in buried talents is our land!	
36.	Автомобиль не роскошь, а средство передвижения. The automobile is not a luxury but a means of transportation.	Народ не роскошь, а средство обогащения. People are not a luxury but a means of getting rich.	Hidden rhyme
37.	Худой мир лучше доброй ссоры Bad peace is better than a good quarrel; similar to the English proverb, *A bad compromise is better than a good lawsuit.*	Худой «Мир» лучше доброго «Челленджера». Bad "Mir" is better than good "Challenger."	Defeated expectancy based on homonymy
38.	Редкая птица долетит до середины Днепра. It is a rare bird that can fly till the middle of the Dnepr river.	Редкий премьер долетит до середины Атлантики. It is a rare prime-minister that can fly till the middle of the Atlantic ocean.	New lexical content of the same syntactic structure
39.	Зачем вы, девочки, красивых любите? 	Почему вы девушки, красивых любите? 	Change of one word

	Why do you, girls, love handsome guys?	For how much you, girls, love handsome guys?	
40.	*Любовь нечаянно нагрянет, когда ее совсем не ждешь.* Loves comes suddenly, when you do not expect it at all.	*Любовь нечаянно нагрянет, когда жену совсем не ждешь.* Love comes suddenly, when you do not expect your wife at all.	Change of one word
41.	*Что бродишь, гармонь, одиноко?* Why do you wander, accordion, all alone?	*Что ты бродишь, гормон одинокий?* Why do you wander, hormone, all alone?	Paronymy
42a.	*Любви все возрасты покорны.* Any age is obedient to love.	*В любви все возрасты проворны.* Any age is quick in love.	Hidden rhyme
42b.		*Любви все плоскости покорны.* Any flat surface will do for love.	Change of one word
43.	*Здравствуй, племя молодое, незнакомое!* Greetings to the young unknown generation!	*Здравствуй, тело молодое, незнакомое!* Greetings to the young unknown body!	Change of one word
44.	*Что посеешь,*	*Что посмеешь,*	Double hidden

144

	то и пожнешь. As you sow you shall mow; similar to the English proverb, *As you sow you shall reap.*	*то и пожмешь.* As you dare you shall grasp.	rhyme
45.	*Сколько лет, сколько зим!* So many summers, so many winters!	*Сколько Лен, сколько Зин!* So many Lenas, so many Zinas!	Paronymy
46.	*Своя рубашка ближе к телу.* Your own shirt is closer to your body.	*Своя Наташка ближе к телу.* Your own Natashka is closer to your body.	Hidden rhyme
47.	*Не в свои сани не садись.* Do not get into someone else's sledge.	*Не на свою Саню не ложись.* Do not lie on someone else's Sanya.	Hidden rhyme, paronymy
48.	*Не место красит человека, а человек место.* It is not the place that adorns the man, but the man who adorns the place.	*Не одежда красит девушку, а отсутствие оной!* It is not the clothes that adorn the girl, but their absence!	New lexical content of the same syntactic structure
49.	*Любовь зла, полюбишь и козла.* Love is cruel; one	*Любовь зла, уснул – и уползла.* Love is cruel: [I]	Hidden rhyme, internal rhyme

	can fall in love even with a goat. This proverb is similar in its meaning to the English proverb *Love is blind.*	fell asleep and [she] disappeared.	
50.	*Близок локоть, да не укусишь.* Close is the elbow, but [you] cannot bite it.	*Близок локоть, да не коленка.* Close is the elbow, but [it is] not a knee.	Defeated expectancy, based on contextual antonyms
51.	*Нас голыми руками не возьмешь.* One cannot catch us with bare hands.	*Девиз холостяка: Нас голыми ногами не возьмешь.* Bachelor's motto: One cannot catch us with naked legs.	Polysemy, extension
52.	*Что у трезвого на уме, то у пьяного на языке.* What the sober man thinks about, the drunken man will say.	*Что у женщины на уме, то мужчине не по карману.* What the woman thinks about, the man cannot afford.	New lexical content of the same syntactic structure
53.	*Бомбы два раза в одно место дважды не падают.* Bombs do not fall into the same place twice.	*Секс-бомбы в одну кровать дважды не падают.* Sex-bombs do not fall into the same bed twice.	New lexical content of the same syntactic structure

54.	*Не хлебом единым жив человек!* Man shall not live on bread alone!	*Не водкой единой пьян человек!* Man shall not get drunk by vodka alone!	New lexical content of the same syntactic structure
55.	*Человеку свойственно ошибаться.* To err is human.	*Человеку свойственно нажираться.* To get drunk is human.	Hidden rhyme
56.	*Кто к нам с мечом придет, тот от меча и погибнет.* He who will come to us with the sword will perish by the sword.	*Кто к нам с пивом придет, тот за водкой и побежит.* He who will come to us with beer will go to bring vodka.	New lexical content of the same syntactic structure
57.	*Эх, не перевелись еще на Руси богатыри – добры молодцы!* (There are still enough bogatyri [worriers] in Russia!	*Эх, не перепились еще на Руси богатыри – добры молодцы!* There are still enough sober worriers in Russia!	Hidden rhyme
58.	*Повинную голову меч не сечет.* A guilty head will not be hit by the sword.	*Похмельную голову меч не сечет.* A drunken head will not be hit by the sword.	Hidden rhyme

59.	*Чему быть, того не миновать.* What is destined to happen, one cannot avoid.	*Чего пить, того не миновать.* What is to be drunk, one cannot avoid.	Hidden rhyme
60.	*Бытие определяет сознание.* Being determines consciousness.	*Питие определяет сознание.* Drinking determines consciousness.	Hidden rhyme
61.	*Рожденный ползать летать не может.* He who was born to crawl will not be able to fly.	*Рожденный строить не пить не может.* He who was born to build cannot but drink.	New lexical content of the same syntactic structure
62.	*Он сказал: «Поехали!» И взмахнул рукой.* He said: Let's go! And waved his hand.	*Он сказал: «Поехали!» И запил водой.* He said: Let's go! And washed it down with water.	Polysemy, hidden rhyme
63.	*Спрайт – не дай себе засохнуть!* Sprite – do not allow yourself to thirst!	*Русская водка – не дай себе просохнуть.* Russian vodka – do not allow yourself to sober.	Hidden rhyme
64.	*Учиться никогда не поздно.* It is never too late to learn.	*Лечиться никогда не поздно.* It is never too late to be treated	Hidden rhyme

148

		[by a physician].	
65.	*Что с возу упало, то пропало.* What has dropped off the cart is lost. This proverb is similar to the English saying, *A mill cannot grind with water that is past.*	*Что с возрастом упало – то пропало.* What has dropped with age is lost.	Paronymy
66.	*Горбатого могила исправит.* A person with a hump will be cured by the grave.	*Горбатого медкомиссия исправит.* A person with a hump will be cured by medical examiners.	Change of one word
67.	*Тяжело в учении, легко в бою.* It is difficult in training, [but] it is easy in combat.	*Тяжело в лечении, легко в гробу.* It is difficult in treatment, [but] it is easy in the coffin.	Double hidden rhyme
68.	*Иных уж нет, а те далече.* Some are gone, and others are far away.	*Иных уж нет, а тех долечат.* Some are gone, and others will be cured [till they die].	Hidden rhyme based on paronymy.
69.	*Мусор из избы не выносить.*	*Мусора, из избы не выносить.*	Syntactic restructuring,

	Do not carry your garbage out of the house.	Cops, do not carry [me] out of the house.	homonymy
70.	*Не поминайте лихом!* Don't think badly of me!	*Не поминайте лохом.* Don't think of me as a *loh*.	Change of one word
71.	*Не свисти – денег не будет.* Do not whistle [in the house] – there will be no money.	*Не свисти – девок не будет.* Do not whistle – there will be no girls.	Paronymy
72a.	*Одна голова хорошо, а две – лучше.* One head is good, but two are better.	*Одна голова хорошо, а две головы – урод.* One head is good, but two are a monster.	Defeated expectancy based on polysemy
72b		*Одна голова хорошо, а с телом – лучше!* One head is good, but with the body is better!	Defeated expectancy based on polysemy
73.	*Весь мир театр, а люди в нем актеры.* All the world is a stage, and people are actors.	*Весь мир театр, а люди в нем вахтеры.* All the world is a stage, and people are door-keepers.	Hidden rhyme
74.	*Унылая пора,*	*Унылая, пора!*	Syntactic re-

150

	(очей очарова-нье!). Melancholy time, (so charming to the eye!)	Melancholy, [it is] time [to go]!	structuring, homonymy
75.	*Оставь надеж-ду всяк сюда входящий.* Leave hope anyone entering here.	*Оставь одежду всяк сюда вхо-дящий!* Leave clothes anyone entering here!	Hidden rhyme
76.	*Ничто не це-нится так до-рого и не обхо-дится так де-шево, как веж-ливость.* Nothing is valued so highly and is given to us so cheaply as po-liteness.	*Ничто не дает-ся нам так де-шево, как хо-чется.* Nothing is given to us as cheaply as we would like.	Defeated ex-pectancy based on syntactic restructuring
77.	*Уходя, гасите свет.* When leaving, switch off the lights.	*Уходя, гасите всех.* When leaving, eliminate every-one.	Polysemy, par-onymy

Pattern III: Extension of the Traditional Proverb

	Traditional Proverb	Anti-Proverb	Language Mechanism
78.	*Всех денег не заработаешь* One cannot earn all the money.	*Всех денег не заработаешь – часть придется украсть.* One cannot earn all the money – some money will have to be stolen.	Defeated expectancy based on the new lexical content
79.	*Деньги не пахнут.* Money has no smell.	*Деньги не пахнут, потому что их отмывают.* Money has no smell, because it is laundered.	Polysemy (twice)
80.	*Не свисти – денег не будет.* Do not whistle [in the house] – there will be no money.	*И только работники ГИБДД опровергают фразу: «Не свисти – денег не будет».* And only traffic police refute the phrase: "Do not whistle – there will be no money."	Polysemy
81.	*Деньги – зло.* Money is evil.	*Наши деньги в 28,66 раза меньшее зло, чем доллары.* Our money is 28.66 times smaller evil than dollars.	Polysemy

82.	*Поддержите отечествен-ного произво-дителя* Support Russian producers!	*Девушки! Не хо-дите замуж за иностранца, под-держите отече-ственного произ-водителя!* Girls! Do not merry foreigners! Support the Russian pro-ducers!	Polysemy
83.	*Граждане россияне! Бе-регите приро-ду!* Citizens of Russia! Protect nature!	*Граждане рос-сияне! Берегите природу родины, отдыхайте на Кипре!* Citizens of Russia! Protect the nature of your motherland, spend vacations in Cypress.	Defeated ex-pectancy, based on the new lexical content
84.	*Обещанного три года ждут.* One has to wait for three years for something that has been prom-ised.	*Обещанного три года ждут. А там снова выборы.* One has to wait for three years for something that has been promised. And then it is time for new elections.	Polysemy
85.	*Искусство требует жертв.* Art requires sacrifices.	*Больше всего жертв требует военное искусство.* Military art re-quires most sacri-fices.	Polysemy

153

86.	*Где раки зи-мvют.* Where crayfish spend winters.	*Там, где раки только зимуют, мы живем круг-лый год.* Where crayfish spend only winters we live all the year round.	Polysemy
87.	*Дуракам закон не писан.* Fools recognize no laws.	*Дуракам закон не писан. А если пи-сан, то не читан. А если читан, то не понят. А если понят, то не так.* Fools recognize no laws. And if they recognize them, they have not read them. And even if they have read them, they have not understood them. And if they have understood them, they understood them in the wrong way.	Anadiplosis
88.	*Лежачего не бьют.* One should not hit a person lying on the ground.	*Никогда не бей лежачего: ведь он может встать.* Never hit a person lying on the ground: he may stand up.	Defeated ex-pectancy based on the new lexical content
89.	*Народ без-молвствует.*	*Народ безмол-вствует все гром-*	Oxymoron

	The people are silent.	*че.* The people are silent louder and louder.	
90.	*Какой же русский не любит быстрой езды!* What Russian is not fond of driving fast!	*Какой же новый русский не любит быстрой езды?* *Сказал гаишник, пересчитывая бабки.* What new Russian is not fond of driving fast, said the policemen counting the money.	Defeated expectancy based on the new lexical content; wellerism
91.	*Титаник напоролся на айсберг.* The Titanic was hit by an iceberg.	*Эх, Аврора, где же был твой айсберг?* Avrora, where was your iceberg?	New lexical content
92.	*У любви свои законы.* Love has its own laws.	*У любви свои законы, но чаще всего там беспредел.* Love has its own laws, but most often it has no laws at all.	Contextual antonymy
93.	*Пристал как банный лист.* [Someone] has stuck like a bath-house leaf.	*Мужчина как банный лист: сначала он пристает к женщине, а потом смывается.*	Polysemy (twice)

		Men are like bath-house leaves: first they stick (pester) to the women, then they wash off (disappear).	
94.	*… на дороге не валяется* [something or someone] does not just lie on the road.	*Хорошие мужики на дороге не валяются. Они валяются на диване.* Valuable men do not just lie on the road. They lie on the sofa.	Defeated expectancy based on polysemy
95.	*Настоящий мужчина должен посадить дерево, построить дом и вырастить сына.* A true man must plant a tree, build a house, and raise a son.	*Настоящая женщина должна спилить дерево, разрушить дом и вырастить дочь.* A true woman must cut the tree, demolish the house and raise a daughter.	Contextual antonymy
96.	*С милым рай и в шалаше.* With my darling, it is paradise even in the shelter made of branches.	*С милым рай и в шалаше, если милый атташе.* With my darling, it is paradise even in the shelter made of branches, if my darling is an attaché.	Internal rhyme

№			
97.	*Любви все возрасты покорны.* Any age is obedient to love.	*Любви все возрасты покорны, но только органы не все.* Any age is obedient to love, but not any organ.	Contextual antonymy
98.	*Любите книгу – источник знаний.* Love the book – the source of knowledge.	*Любите жену – надежный источник знаний ваших недостатков.* Love the wife – the reliable source of knowledge about your shortcomings.	New lexical content
99a.	*Дети – цветы жизни.* Children are flowers of life.	*Дети – цветы жизни. Дарите девушкам цветы* Children are flowers of life. Give flowers to girls.	Polysemy
99b.		*Дети – цветы жизни. На могиле родителей.* Children are flowers of life. On the grave of the parents.	Polysemy
100.	*В вине мудрость.* In wine there is wisdom. This is a Russian translation of the old Latin	*В вине мудрость, в пиве – сила, в воде – микробы.* In wine there is wisdom, in beer – power, in water – microbes.	New lexical content

	maxim, *In vino veritas.*		
101.	*Водка наш враг.* Vodka is our enemy.	*Водка наш враг. А мы врагов не боимся.* Vodka is our enemy. But we are not afraid of enemies.	Polysemy
102.	*Алкоголь в малых дозах безвреден.* Alcohol in small doses is harmless.	*Алкоголь в малых дозах безвреден в любом количестве.* Alcohol in small doses is harmless in any quantities.	Oxymoron
103a	*Здоровье не купишь.* One cannot buy health.	*Здоровье не купишь, хватило бы на лекарства.* One cannot buy health; you will be lucky to have enough money for medicine only.	Polysemy
103b		*Здоровье уже можно купить, но еще не на что.* One can now buy health, but there is no money yet.	Polysemy
104.	*Дорога ложка к обеду.* A spoon is important by din-	*Дорога к обеду ложка, а к инфаркту – неотложка.*	Internal rhyme

158

	ner time.	A spoon is important by dinner time, and ambulance – by the heart attack time.	
105.	*Необходимо вовремя обращаться к врачу.* It is necessary to visit with your doctor in time.	*Если болезнь не начать вовремя лечить – она может пройти сама.* If we do not start to treat a disease in due time it can pass itself.	Defeated expectancy based on the new lexical content
106.	*Предупреждать болезни легче, чем лечить.* To prevent a disease is easier than to treat it.	*Предупреждать болезни легче, чем лечить. А лечить прибыльнее, чем предупреждать.* To prevent a disease is easier than to treat it. And to treat it is more profitable than to prevent it.	Chiasmus
107.	*Курить вредно* Smoking is bad for your health.	*Курить вредно, пить противно, а умирать здоровым – жалко.* Smoking is bad, drinking is disgusting, but dying healthy is a pity.	Defeated expectancy based on the new lexical content
108.	*Богатый внутренний*	*Хирурги считают, что внутренний*	Polysemy

	мир. Rich inner world.	*мир человека луч- ше всего раскры- вается на опера- ционном столе.* Surgeons believe that the inner world of a person is best revealed on the op- eration table.	
109.	*Молитва – это разговор с Богом.* Prayer is a talk with God.	*Когда ты гово- ришь с Богом – это молитва. Ко- гда Бог с тобой – это шизофрения.* When you talk to God, this is a prayer. When God talks to you, this is schizophrenia.	Chiasmus
110.	*Время лечит.* Time cures. This proverb is similar to the English one, *Time cures all things.*	*Время лечит, но за деньги быст- рее.* Time cures, but for money it is quicker.	Polysemy
111.	*Вешать лапшу на уши.* To hang pasta on ears.	*Если вам вешают лапшу на уши, требуйте, чтобы она была высоко- го качества.* If someone hangs pasta on your ears, require it to be of the high quality.	Polysemy

160

160

112.	*Враг не дрем-лет.* The enemy is not dozing.	*Враг не дремлет – он спит.* The enemy is not dozing – he is sleeping.	Defeated expectancy based on polysemy
113a	*Не в деньгах счастье.* Happiness is not in money.	*Не в деньгах сча-стье, а в их коли-честве.* Happiness is not in money, but in the amount of money.	Defeated expectancy based on the new lexical content
113b		*Верю, что не в деньгах счастье, но хочется убе-диться самому.* I believe that happiness is not in money, but I would like to check it out myself.	Defeated expectancy based on the new lexical content
114.	*От сумы да от тюрьмы не зарекайся.* No one can be sure that he will not be poor or get in jail.	*От сумы да от тюрьмы не заре-кайся, – говорит кенгуру в зоопар-ке.* No one can be sure that he will not be poor or get in jail, said the kangaroo in the zoo.	Polysemy, me-tonymy; wellerism
115.	*Самогон ваш враг.* Samogon [home-made vodka] is your	*Самогон ваш враг. Гоните его!* Samogon is your enemy. Drive it away!	Polysemy

	enemy.		
116.	*Гоняться за женщинами.* To chase women.	*Мужчина гоняется за женщиной, пока она его не поймает.* A man is chasing a woman until she catches him.	Oxymoron
117.	*Собака – друг человека.* A dog is a man's friend. The same proverb exists in English, *A dog is a man's best friend.*	*Хорошо, когда собака – друг, но плохо, когда друг – собака.* It is good when your dog is a friend, but it is bad when your friend is a dog.	Chiasmus
118.	*Старость приносит мудрость.* Old age brings wisdom.	*Старость не всегда приносит мудрость. Иногда старость приходит одна.* Old age does not always bring wisdom. Sometimes old age comes alone.	Polysemy
119.	*Труд сделал из обезьяны человека.* Labor has made the man out of the ape.	*Работа сделала из обезьяны человека, а из женщины – лошадь.* Labor has made the man out of the ape, and the horse out of the woman.	Polysemy

120.	*Хорошо там, где нас нет* It is good where we are not. Cf. the English proverb, *Grass is always greener on the other side of the fence.*	*Хорошо там, где нас нет. Но теперь, когда мы везде, где может быть хорошо?* It is good where we are not. But now, when we are everywhere, where can it be good?	Defeated expectancy based on the new lexical content
121.	*Янки, гоу хоум.* Yankee, go home.	*Янки, гоу хоум, и меня с собой возьмите.* Yankee, go home and take me with you.	Defeated expectancy based on the new lexical content
122.	*В России две беды: дураки и дороги.* There are two problems in Russia: fools and roads.	*В России две беды: дураки и дороги, а в Америке две радости – умники и бездорожье.* There are two problems in Russia: fools and roads, while in America there are two good things: clever people and lack of roads.	Contextual antonyms

Pattern IV: New Form – New Wisdom

	Anti-Proverb	Language Mechanism
123.	*Вобла – это кит, доживший до коммунизма.* Vobla [Caspian roach] is a whale that has lived until communism.	New lexical content
124.	*Раздельное питание – это когда народ и власть питаются отдельно.* Separate diet – this is when the people and the government eat separately.	Polysemy
125.	*У плохого студента есть шанс стать хорошим солдатом.* A bad student has a chance to become a good soldier.	Contextual antonymy
126.	*Мы все стоим у черты бедности – правда, по разные ее стороны.* We all stand at the poverty line, but on the opposite sides of it.	Polysemy
127.	*Социальное расслоение – это когда на одних ушах золото, а на других – лапша.* Social differentiation – it is when on some ears there is gold, on others – pasta.	Polysemy
128.	*Если народ терпит слишком долго, его страна превращается в дом терпимости.* If the people suffer too long, their country becomes the house of	Homonymy

164

	sufferance.	
129.	*Если бы не народ, у правительства не было бы никаких проблем.* But for the people, the government will not have any problems.	New lexical content
130.	*После того, что правительство сделало с народом, оно обязано на нем жениться.* After what the government has done to the people, the government should merry them.	Polysemy
131.	*Беда Москвы в том, что она со всех сторон окружена Россией.* The problem with Moscow is that it is surrounded by Russia from all sides.	New lexical content
132.	*Скольких товарищей потеряли мы на пути в господа!* How many comrades have we lost on our way to misters!	Polysemy
133.	*Что у нас хорошо организовано, так это преступность.* The thing that is well-organized in our country is crime.	Polysemy
134.	*Пессимист изучает китайский язык, оптимист – английский, реалист – автомат Калашникова.* Pessimists study Chinese, optimists study English, realists – Kalashnikov machine-gun.	Defeated expectancy, based on the new lexical content

135.	*Лучший выход из российского кризиса – Шереметьево-2.* The best way out of the Russian crisis is Sheremetyevo-2.	Polysemy
136.	*Счастье – иметь красивую жену, а горе – иметь такое счастье.* It is a good fortune to have a beautiful wife, and it is a misfortune to have such good fortune.	Polysemy, contextual antonymy
137.	*Меняю рай в шалаше на ад во дворце.* I will change the paradise in the shelter of branches for the hell in the palace.	Antonymy
138.	*От любви умирают редко, зато рождаются часто.* Because of love, people seldom die, but often are born.	Polysemy
139.	*Свадьба – это контрольный выстрел Амура.* Wedding is the control shot of Amor.	Metaphor
140.	*Любая юбка лучше всего смотрится на спинке стула.* Any skirt looks best of all on the back of the chair.	Defeated expectancy based on the new lexical content
141.	*Самый лучший способ запомнить день рождения жены – один раз его забыть.* The best way to remember your wife's birthday is to forget it once.	Oxymoron

142.	*Больному стало легче – он перестал дышать.* The patient felt better – he stopped breathing.	Defeated expectancy based on the new lexical content
143.	*Как врачи его ни лечили, он все равно выздоровел.* No matter how the doctors tried to treat him, the patient recovered.	Defeated expectancy based on oxymoron
144.	*Больной, просыпайтесь! Пора принимать снотворное!* Patient, wake up! It's time to take your sleeping pills!	Oxymoron
145.	*О вреде курения пишут так много, что я твердо решил бросить читать.* There are so many books about the harm of smoking that I decided to give up reading.	Defeated expectancy based on new lexical content
146.	*Склероз вылечить нельзя, зато о нем можно забыть.* Sclerosis cannot be cured, but one can forget about it.	Contextual antonymy
147.	*Чистая совесть свидетельствует о начале склероза.* Clear conscience means the beginning of sclerosis.	New lexical content
148.	*Каждая трава – лекарственная, надо только подобрать под нее болезнь.* Each herb has medicinal value; one just needs to find a corresponding disease.	Defeated expectancy based on the new lexical content

149.	Сами *подумайте, откуда у вас при вашем образе жизни и зар-плате, могут быть хорошие анализы?* Just think about it yourself, how can you, with your way of life and your salary, have good test results?	New lexical content
150.	*Почему так распространено отложение солей? А больше ничего отложить не удается.* Why the deposition of salts is so common today? Because this is the only thing one can deposit.	Polysemy
151.	*Встречи без галстуков позво-ляют больше заложить за во-ротник.* Meetings without ties allow putting more behind the collar.	Polysemy (twice)
152.	*Если тебя послали за пивом, значит, тебе доверяют!* If you are sent to bring beer, it means that you are trusted!	New lexical content
153.	*Если вы проснулись на улице, значит, вы там заснули.* If you woke up in the street, it means you fell asleep there.	Defeated expectancy based on the new lexical content
154.	*Пока выбьешь место под солн-цем, уже вечер.* By the time you elbow your place under the sun, it is evening already.	Polysemy
155.	*Если у вас нет проблем, зна-*	New lexical con-

	чит, вы уже умерли. If you do not have any problems it means you have died already.	tent
156.	*Чтобы сохранить ангельский характер, нужно дьявольское терпение.* To have angelic character one needs diabolic patience.	Polysemy and antonymy
157.	*Человека хоронят два ящика – гроб и телевизор.* Humans are buried with the help of two boxes: a casket and a TV.	Polysemy

Notes

[1] See, for example: Mieder, Wolfgang. *Proverbs: A Handbook.* Greenwood Press, 2004.
[2] Incidentally, the same wisdom is expressed in modern computer slang, in a well-known acronym GIGO (garbage in, garbage out: if you give computer bad data, do not expect the machine to provide you with reliable results of calculations).
[3] In September 1999, when still being prime-minister of Russia, Putin said:

> "Russian airplanes are striking and will continue striking the bases of terrorists in Chechnya, and this will continue no matter where terrorists might be. We will follow the terrorists everywhere, if in the airport, then it will be in the airport. So, we will, if you excuse me, catch them in the outhouse, we will kill them there, eventually. That is all, the question is closed."

The statement immediately acquired proverbial status, and is known to literally any person in Russia. So there is no doubt that it was not only coined very well, but the timing of it was good for it to attain the level of folk wisdom. One aspect of this expression is especially worth noting, as it will become a standard feature of *putinspeak*: it uses prison slang, as in Russian the word which means "kill" is taken from the language of criminals ("mochit"). This was the first but not the last time when Putin all of a sudden used prison slang in his speeches or his answers to journalists' questions.
[4] It should be kept in mind that this and many similar antiproverbs that mention US currency were coined during the time when the dollar was the absolute leader in the world, and the euro either did not exist yet or was not important. Now (2008), of course, the situation has changed, and US currency is not valued as highly in the world as it used to. In fact, most Russian citizens and companies use euros today in their business matters.
[5] As a general rule, Russian computer slang uses Russian transliteration of the English term, or replaces the English word with a Russian word that sounds the same but has little if any connec-

tion to the original word. For example, *хакер* (hacker), *фича* (feature), *батон* (button, literally, *loaf*); *мыло* (email, literally, *soap*), etc.

[6] This aspect of life in modern Russia was used as the basis for a sad joke in a popular TV show *Городок* (Little Town). Two high school friends who have not met for a long time meet by accident in the street. One has become a new Russian, the other is a bum. The bum seeing that his old friend is so successful tells him, "I have not eaten anything for six days!" – clearly hoping that the rich guy will give him some money. The new Russian interprets this in his own way (it cannot occur to him that his old friend cannot afford to buy food) and says: "You have to force yourself to eat, even if you do not want to."

[7] Hence, another sad joke dating back to the late 80s, where the situation with food supplies was the worst: A customer comes to a grocery store and asks, "Can you weigh half a kilo of food?" The shop-assistant answers, "Sure, we can. Bring the food [and we will weigh it for you]."

[8] It is possible that this coinage reflects an incident that happened to Boris Eltsin, the first president of Russia, on September 28, 1989 (this was still during the Soviet Union time) when he fell from a bridge not far from his dacha near Moscow. There are different versions of this episode; according to one of them, some strangers put a sack on his head and pushed him into the water; this was inter-preted as an attempt of the communist party leaders to discredit Eltsin for his views and actions. This sounds like a line from a detective story, but is in fact quite possible: Eltsin was openly criticizing many things, and in general was good at demolishing the old establishment, though his own views were those of a populist.

[9] Alexander Suvorov did not lose a single battle during his military career. He is also the author of several books on the art of war, including his famous "The Science of Victory." It is not by chance that one of the highest military awards instituted in the Soviet Union during WWII was named after Suvorov.

[10] And a show it was: there was only one candidate for every "elected" position, so all the voters had to do was to obediently vote for that candidate. Of course, in theory one could vote against the one candidate on the ballot, but in reality it seldom

happened, and even if it did happen, it did not change anything: the vast majority of people will passively "vote" for the candidate offered to them by the authorities.

Incidentally, after democratic elections were re-established in Russia in the early 90-s, quite a few changes for the worse took place, as well. For example, during the presidency of Vladimir Putin, elections of governors were abolished and now they are appointed by the president with the approval of local legislatures.

[11] In this play Pushkin describes one of the most dramatic moments in the history of Russia. Boris Godunov was the tsar of Russia during 1598-1605. Godunov's career began at the court of Ivan the Terrible. When Ivan the Terrible died, his son Feodor became the tsar, but Feodor was feeble both in mind and in health, so Boris became de facto regent of Russia since 1584. Ivan the Terrible had another son (born from his seventh wife Maria Nagaya) who died at the age of ten in 1591 (there was a rumor that he was assassinated). There was also a rumor that Dmitry did not die but was hiding. This allowed several imposters to claim that they were the youngest son of Ivan the Terrible who had escaped assassination. Many people believed that, and thus False Dmitriy I became the tsar in 1605, after Boris Godunov mysteriously died. This marked the beginning of the so-called Time of Troubles in Russia.

[12] And this is not a figure of speech anymore: it is common knowledge that free press and other media have disappeared in Russia during the presidency of Vladimir Putin; all the major TV stations and newspapers are controlled by the government, and express only the official point of view. The only medium that is left for independent journalists is the Internet, but this is of no importance, as comparatively few people have Internet access in Russia.

[13] Blok uses this proverb twice in his poem, first in Latin, and later, in the end, in Russian. Here is the stanza with the original proverb:

А рядом, у соседних столиков
Лакеи сонные торчат,
И пьяницы с глазами кроликов
"In vino veritas!" кричат.

172

[14] For example, during 1940-1976 the production of alcoholic drinks increased 6.3 times (*USSR Economy during 60 Years. Annual Statistical Report*. Moscow, 1977, p.508). During the same time, the population of the USSR increased from 159, 153,000 in 1940 to 257, 824,000 in 1977 (ibid, p. 42); thus, only 1.6 times. Consequently, the production of alcohol per capita increased 3.9 times.

[15] When the soviet government (during the early 80s) tried to restrict alcohol sales and use other administrative means to force people not to drink (raise prices), there appeared a folk verse:

Водка стала пять и восемь
Все равно мы пить не бросим
Передайте Ильичу
Нам и десять по плечу.
Если станет двадцать пять
Будем Зимний брать опять.

(Vodka now costs five and eight [rubles a bottle]/ but we will not stop drinking/ Tell Ilyich [Brezhnev]/ that we can afford even 10 rubles/ But if it costs 25/ we will take Zimniy [palace, the seat of the government seized during the socialist revolution of 1917] again).

[16] Cf. a popular joke: How much is one drop of cognac? – Nothing. – Then please fill my glass with drops.

[17] See: Engels, Friedrich. "The Part Played by Labor in the Transition from Ape to Man." 1876. 25 August 2008 <http:// www. marxists.org/archive/marx/works/1876/part-played-labour/index. htm>.

[18] Nikolay Karamzin is the author of the first history of Russia – *Istoriya gosudarstva rossiyskogo* (History of the Russian State) published in 1815.

[19] As usual, folk wisdom reacted to the situation in a short and witty (though of course very sad) joke: Brezhnev is asked a question, "Why is there nothing to eat during the transition from socialism to communism?" He answers, "But nobody promised to feed you on the way!"

[20] One has to have lived in the Soviet Union to understand that completely, but let me give you a testimony of a famous literary

figure, Benedict Sarnov. In his book *Наш советский новояз*
(Our Soviet Newspeak. Moscow, 2002) he describes the following episode.

An elderly person, who has lived all his life during the soviet
regime, went to Germany to visit his daughter who was living
there. She took him to a grocery store in her neighborhood; the
father was impressed, but when they left the store he told her,
"Well, this is fine of course, but now show me a regular store." It
could not occur to him that a store that had so many food choices
was a regular one – in his mind, this could happen only in the
closed store for *nomenklatura*. The daughter never managed to
persuade him that it was not a special store – he remained in his
opinion that she was lying to him in order to show how well off
her life was (Sarnov 154).

Now, of course, this system is gone, but the divide between
the *haves* and *have nots* is still here; in fact, it got worse, only
now the new Russians and government officials are separated
from the common people not so much by their closed chain of
special services (though they still exist) but by the amount of
money they have. So as long as some people can hardly make
ends meet and cannot afford to buy the bare necessities, while
some others buy football clubs, mansions in Florida and ocean
yachts, this anti-proverb has good chances to stay in the language for a long time.

[21] For example, 25% of the population of the Republic of Karelia
(one of the subjects of the Russian Federation) is eligible for free
legal aid (these data were provided by the Karelian state bureau
of legal aid). Today the population of Karelia is about 693,000
people; thus, 25% is over 173,000 people. To be eligible for legal aid one has to have no more than 5,000 rubles (about $213)
per month. It means that a quarter of the population has no more
than 5,000 rubles per month. Just to give an idea how little
money it is: a liter of gas costs over 25 rubles (that is 4 dollars
per gallon) (summer 2008); if an average tank is 40 liters
(roughly 10 gallons) to fill the tank one needs 1,000 rubles; so to
fill an average 20-gallon tank of an American vehicle, one will
need 2,000 rubles.

[22] According to Mercer's 2008 Worldwide Cost of Living Survey, Moscow was rated the most expensive city in the world in

174

2008 (42% higher than New York, the most expensive city in the US). See: <http://www.forbes.com/2008/07/23/cities-expensive-world-forbeslife-cx_zg_0724expensivecities.html>

[23] Cf. a popular inside joke of the medical doctors: Shall we treat him or let him live?

[24] At its Second Congress in 1905, the future communist party of Russia (it was called social-democratic party then) split into two fractions: Bolsheviks ("the majority") and Mensheviks ("the minority"). The Bolsheviks eventually became the ruling party after the revolution, so in practical terms, this word became a synonym to a communist in Russia.

[25] The socialist revolution in Russia took place on October 25, 1917 – hence, it is usually referred to as the October revolution. In those days Russia was using the Julian calendar, while most of the European countries by that time had adopted the Gregorian calendar. On January 1st, 1918, Russia adopted the new calendar, too, and what used to be October 25 became November 7 (the difference between the two systems was 12 days by then). Thus, the October revolution was celebrated on the 7th of November. Incidentally, the Russian Orthodox Church refused to accept the new calendar; thus, it still celebrates Christmas on January 7.

[26] The Supreme Soviet of the USSR was officially the highest organ of power. Its deputies were elected (by means of special quotas) from all layers of the society, with the emphasis on representatives of workers and peasants – the two main "ruling" classes in the Soviet Union.

[27] Lenin. His full name is Vladimir Ilyich Lenin; and the patronymic was often used to express the emotional attitude towards this person.

[28] Of the communist party. Since there was only one political party in the USSR, it was not necessary to give the full name, as any organ (regional, republican, central committee) could only be a committee of the Communist Party of the Soviet Union. This led to an important change in the meaning of these (and many other words): their meaning got narrower.

[29] Semen Budenniy (1883-1973) was one of the famous soviet military commanders during the Civil War (1918-1920) in soviet Russia.

[30] Saint-Petersburg.

[31] Nikolay Yudenich (1862-1933) – one of the military commanders of the White Army during the Civil war of 1918-1920. He was leading the attack of white forces on Saint-Petersburg in October and November of 1919, which resulted in the defeat of the White Army. Since 1920 he lived abroad.

[32] Well-to-do peasants, private land owners, as opposed to collective farmers.

[33] As many other propaganda slogans, this one had nothing to do with reality: when in the 1920s-30s the communist party started to organize collective farms by force, and the backbone of Russian agriculture – well-to-do peasants who produced enough grain for Russia to even import it – were physically exterminated or exiled to Siberia, the great hunger began which resulted in the deaths of millions of people. The worst years were1932-1933: according to various sources, between two and four million people died. The Russian Duma (parliament) in a special statement "To the Memory of the Victims of Hunger on the Territory of the USSR in the 1930s" passed on April 2, 2008, estimates that the number of people died was even greater – seven million.

[34] See note #24 about *kulaki*. In fact, in reality it was the other way round: collective farms could not compete with them.

[35] Those interested in learning more about Cockney rhyming slang can be referred to the latest Cockney dictionary: Franklyn, J.A. *Dictionary of Rhyming Slang*. London, 1969.

[36] It is not easy to give any reliable numbers. Official statistics claims that in 2005 18% of the citizens of Russia lived below the poverty line, in 2008 this number allegedly is 14%. This does not look so bad, but one has to keep in mind what is meant by poverty line (minimum living wage) in Russia. In 2008 it was set by the Russian government at 3,879 rubles per month. See the official Russian government newspaper *Rossiyskaya gazeta*: <http://www.rg.ru/2008/02/09/prozhit-minimum-anons.html>.

What one can buy with this money was exemplified in note 18 above. That is why many people believe that the percentage of people who de facto live below the poverty line (though ac-

176

cording to the official statistics they do not) is much higher. Of course, the situation is different in various parts of Russia: there will be fewer poor people in Moscow than in my native Republic of Karelia, where even by the official statistics a quarter of the population is poor.

[37] There were 15 soviet republics in the Soviet Union, except for a short period of time when there were 16 republics (Karelian-Finnish Soviet Socialist Republic existed between 1940 and 1956; before 1940 and after 1956 it was an administrative region within the Russian Federation – the largest of the 15 republics of the USSR).

Bibliography

Collections of Russian Proverbs

K.G. Bersenyeva. *Russkie poslovitsy i pogovorki* (Russian proverbs and Sayings). Moscow: Tsentrpoligraph, 2005.

Dal, V. I. *Poslovitsy Russkogo Naroda* (Proverbs of the Russian People). Moscow, 2005.

M.I. Dubrovin. *Angliyskiye i russkiye poslovitsy i pogovorki v illustratsiyah* (English and Russian proverbs and Sayings Illustrated). 2nd ed. Moscow: Prosveshcheniye, 1995.

V.P. Felitsina, Yu. E. Prokhorov. *Russkie poslovitsy, pogovorki i krylatye vyrazheniya* Russian proverbs, sayings and famous quotations). 2nd ed. Moscow: Russkiy yazyk, 1988.

Selected Proverbs and Sayings of the Russian people. Ed. A. Prokofiev. Moscow: Hudozhestvennaya literatura, 1957.

Snegirev I. M. *Slovar russkih poslovits i pogovorok* (Dictionary of Russian Proverbs and Sayings). Nizhniy Novgorod: Russkiy kupets, 1996.

Zhukov, V.P. *Slovar russkih poslovits i pogovorok* (Dictionary of Russian Proverbs and Sayings). Moscow: Russkiy yazyk, 1993.

Zimin, V.I., Spirin, A.S. *Poslovitsy i pogovorki russkogo naroda* (Proverbs and Sayings of the Russian People). 3rd ed. Moscow: Feniks, 2006.

Mokienko, Victor et al. *Slovar russkih poslovits* (Dictionary of Russian Proverbs). Moscow: Astrel publishers, 2007.

Zhigulev, A.M. *Russkiye narodniye poslovitsy i pogovorki* (Russian Folk Proverbs and Sayings). Moscow: Moskovskiy rabochiy, 1965.

Collections of Russian Anti-Proverbs

Mokienko V., Nikitina N. *Tolkovy slovar yazyka sovdepii* (Dictionary of the Soviet Language). Saint-Petersburg: Saint-Petersburg University press, 1998.

Mokienko V., Walter, H. *Pricolny slovar* (Dictionary of Jokes: Anti-Proverbs and Anti-Aphorisms). Saint-Petersburg: Neva Publishers, 2006.

178

Walter, H., Mokienko V. *Anti-poslovitsy russkogo naroda* (Anti-Proverbs of the Russian People). Saint-Petersburg: Neva publishers, 2005.

Collections of Anti-Proverbs in Other Languages

English
Mieder W., Litovkina A. *Twisted Wisdom. Modern Anti-Proverbs.* Burlington: The University of Vermont, 1999.
Litovkina A., Mieder W. *Old Proverbs Never Die – They Just Diversify.* Burlington: The University of Vermont, 2006.

German
Gossler, Erica. *Besser Arm dran als Bein ab. Anti-Sprichworter und ihresgleichen.* Wien: Edition Praesens, 2005.
Mieder, Wolfgang. *Antisprichwörter.* Band I. Wiesbaden: Verlag für deutche Sprache. 1982
Mieder, Wolfgang. *Antisprichwörter.* Band II. Wiesbaden: Verlag für deutche Sprache. 1985.
Mieder, Wolfgang. *Antisprichwörter.* Band III. Wiesbaden: Quelle & Meyer. 1989.

French
Mignaval, Philippe. *Proverbes pour rire – de faux proverbes plus vrais que les vrais.* Paris: Marabout, 2004.

Hungarian
Litovkina, Anna, Vargha, Katalin. *The Nation Lives in Its Jokes. Hungarian Proverb Parodies.* Budapest, 2005.
Litovkina, Anna, Vargha, Katalin. *The Nation Lives in Its Jokes. Selected Proverb Parodies.* Budapest, 2006.

Selected Studies on Anti-Proverbs

Anti-Proverbs. Eds. Anna Litovkina and Carl Lindahl. *Acta Ethnographica Hungarica.* Volume 52, #1, 2007.
Mieder Wolfgang. *Verkehrte Worte: Antizitate aus Literatur and Medien.* Wiesbaden: Quelle & Meyer, 1997.

Mieder Wolfgang. *Verdrehte Weissheiten: Anti-sprichwörter aus Literatur und Medien.* Wiesbaden: Quelle & Meyer, 1998.

Mieder Wolfgang. *Phrasen verdreschen: Antiredensarten aus Literatur und Medien.* Heidelberg: Quelle & Meyer, 1999.

Mieder, Wolfgang. *Proverbs: A Handbook.* Greenwood Press, 2004.

Mieder, Wolfgang. "Anti-proverbs and Mass Communication." *Anti-Proverbs.* Ed. Gabor Barna, 2007. 17-45.

Neumann Siegfried. *Sprichwörtliches aus Mecklenbuirg.* Göttingen: Otto Schwarz & Co, 1996.

Nikolayeva Ye. "Transformirovannye poslovisty kak element sovremennoy smehovoy kultury" (Transformed proverbs as an element of the modern laughing culture). *Nowa frazeologia w nowey Europie. Tezy referatow miedzynarodowej konferencii naukowej.* Greifswald, 2002.

Valdaeva, T. "Anti-Proverbs or New Proverbs: The Use of English Anti-Proverbs and Their Stylistic Analysis." *Proverbium* 20, 2003. 379-390.

Walter, H., Mokienko V. "Antiposlovitsy v sovremennoy zhivoy russkoy rechi" (Anti-Proverbs in Modern Live Russian Speech). *Anti-poslovitsy russkogo naroda* (Anti-Proverbs of the Russian People). Saint-Petersburg: Neva publishers, 2005. 3-17.

Walter, H., Mokienko V. "Russkie antiposlovisty i ih leksikograficheskoye opisinaye" (Russian Anti-proverbs and their Lexicographical Description). *Anti-Proverbs.* Eds. Anna Litovkina and Carl Lindahl 2007. 157-175.